Knowing Me — Knowing You

Also by Malcolm Goldsmith

Knowing Me — Knowing God

KNOWING ME — KNOWING YOU

Exploring Personality Type and Temperament

MALCOLM GOLDSMITH
and MARTIN WHARTON

For Tom and Kate, and Joanna, Andrew and Mark. They more than anyone else have taught us how to appreciate and value differences in personality.

First published in Great Britain 1993
Society for Promoting Christian Knowledge
Holy Trinity Church
Marylebone Road
London NW1 4DU

British Library Cataloguing-in-Publication Data
A catalogue record for this book is available from the British Library

ISBN 0–281–05721–4

10 9 8 7 6 5 4 3 2 1

Typeset by Latimer Trend, Plymouth
First printed and bound in Great Britain by
Biddles Ltd, Guildford and King's Lynn
Reprinted in Great Britain by Ashford Colour Press

Contents

Foreword *by Peter Briggs Myers*   vii
Introduction   1

PART ONE

1   *Vive la Différence!*   7
2   What's It All About?   12
3   Profiles of the Different Types   41
4   The Beginning, Not the End   62
5   Needing Each Other   72

PART TWO

6   People Living Together   89
7   Teams Working Together   106
8   Learning and Teaching Together   124

PART THREE

9   Looking at the Church   135
10   Type and Spirituality   156

PART FOUR

11   A Bit of Fun for Christmas   185
12   Two Remarkable Women   192

Notes   197

Foreword

It is a pleasure to contribute a Foreword to *Knowing Me — Knowing You* and to commend the authors for a delightful introduction to my mother's work written especially for those coming to it from an interest in, or association with, the Church. Isabel Briggs Myers was not a member of any religious denomination but throughout her life demonstrated a deep and abiding faith in her Creator and a loving concern and respect for all of God's creatures. She was a happy person who felt there was more than enough adversity in the world and she dreamed of helping people to help themselves by concentrating on the positive, by recognizing and appreciating their gifts, and by understanding and valuing human differences. She saw, all around her, people having problems with other people: husbands with wives, parents with children, neighbours with each other, and colleagues in the work place. She recognized that people are different, but refused to accept the commonly-held (at that time) idea that these differences were somehow all deviations from some 'normal' behaviour. She found strengths and admirable characteristics in widely dissimilar personalities, and concluded that the differences she observed could not be satisfactorily explained as deviations or exceptions to *any* conceivable 'normal personality'. People, she reasoned, were simply born with different gifts.

With her mother, Katharine Cook Briggs, she began to explore the differences she observed, and the problems these differences might be creating. My grandmother, Katharine Briggs, had made a start at identifying and giving names to some of these differences in the early 1920s before she came across the English translation of Carl Jung's *Psychological Types*. As she told the story, she 'threw her work into the dustbin' and carried on using the names and concepts formulated by the Swiss psychologist. It is a little ironic that shortly thereafter Jung seemed to lose interest in his theory of psychological type. He was, after all, a practising therapist dealing mainly with healing mentally and spiritually sick people. Ordinary, healthy, 'normal' people didn't come to him and he was not very concerned with the constructive use of 'normal' human differences. His *Psychological Types* is not an easy book to read, and his examples of the behaviour of different types tend to the extreme, in some cases almost to a caricature of type. But his theory was sound and intriguing, and my mother and grandmother made cautious steady progress in relating it to the everyday behaviour of effective, rational, but *different* human beings.

As long as they worked on their own to understand and relate their observations they had no problem, but when in 1943 they produced the first set of questions destined to become the Myers Briggs Type Indicator (MBTI), they came face to face with double-barrelled opposition from the academic community. In the first place, neither of them was a psychologist, neither had an advanced academic degree nor, for that matter, *any* formal training in psychology, statistics, or test construction. Second, the academic community (and even Jungian scholars and analysts at that time) had little use for Jung's theory of psychological type, and therefore even less use for a self-report questionnaire purporting to identify type created by two unknown women who were 'obviously totally unqualified'. As it happened, however, Isabel Myers was not all that unqualified; true, she had no formal academic training in the required disciplines, but she had a first-rate mind and had, for more than a year, apprenticed herself to a man who *was* a qualified expert in the techniques and tools she needed. He was Edward N. Hay, at that time personnel manager of the Philadelphia Company, a large financial bank, and from him she learned what she needed to know about test construction, scoring, validation and statistics.

Undismayed by the lack of interest or acceptance by the psychological community, Isabel Myers concentrated on developing the Indicator: gathering data; refining the questions; and applying the accepted tests for validity, reliability, repeatability and statistical significance. Along the way, she was buoyed up by the enthusiasm and delight of the vast majority of people to whom she administered and explained the Indicator; she called it the 'Ah Ha!' reaction, the expression of delight that so often came with a person's recognition of some aspect of their personality identified by the Indicator. One of her greatest pleasures in giving feedback after scoring a person's Indicator was the occasional astonished response: 'What a relief to find out that it is alright to be *me*!'

Knowing Me — Knowing You is a welcome addition to a series of books that look at Type and the constructive use of human differences from a variety of aspects. It is an excellent introduction to the subject, and may well whet your appetite for further exploration. The authors have identified Isabel Myers' own book about the Indicator, *Gifts Differing*, and a number of additional sources of information and I commend them to you, especially if you are not currently able to experience actually completing and receiving feedback from your own answers to the MBTI. Happily, the opportunities to take one of the legitimate versions of the MBTI (Form G, Form F, the Expanded Analysis Report (EAR), or the Type Differentiation Indicator (TDI)) either as part of a Workshop or individually from a qualified MBTI professional are increasing each month all over the world.

I cherish a personal conviction that much of the non-physical pain and stress in our world is the result of misunderstandings between generally well-intentioned people, and is not occasioned by irreparable disagreements. If this is so, great gains in the quality of everyday life should be possible for each of us through a better understanding of ourselves, of how we gather our information, of how we process it and come to conclusions or decisions, and of how we communicate our thoughts and wishes to others. Greater cooperation and harmony should be possible if we can learn to understand and appreciate the ways in which others differ from ourselves, and can find ways to communicate with others in a fashion they can understand and be comfortable with. Carl Jung spoke of archetypes, the symbols, myths and concepts that appear to be inborn and shared by members of a civilization transcending and not depending on words for communication and recognition. Different cultures may have different forms of their archetypes, but the concepts are universal. If Type is such a concept, and universal across different cultures, different religions, different environments, what a challenge lies before us! It could even be possible for the 'Ah Ha!' experience upon recognizing something about oneself, or the reason for a difference from someone else, to extend across political and economic borders, to bring understanding and respect and acceptance of the differences between people of different nations, races, and persuasions. Isabel Myers, shortly before she died, expressed as her fondest wish that long after she was gone her work would go on helping people to recognize and enjoy their gifts. I think she would be pleased by the increased appreciation of her work in the years after her death. I think she would be pleased by the publication of *Knowing Me — Knowing You.*

Peter Briggs Myers
Washington D.C.

Introduction

There are two reasons why this book has been written. First of all, it has been written as a sign of gratitude to the many men and women who over the years have worked to develop and promote the Myers Briggs Type Indicator® – sometimes against great odds – because for both of us this has been a source of fascination, insight, help and challenge. There is a story in the Gospels of a woman who met Jesus by the side of a well, and after a discussion with him she went back to her village and invited her friends to come and meet this man who told her all about herself. It has been our experience that a great many people attending Myers Briggs Workshops have been enabled to come 'face to face' with themselves in a remarkable and creative way – and we would include ourselves in that number.

Secondly, we have written this book to fill a gap in British publishing and in order to introduce more people to the work and insights of Isabel Briggs Myers. We both run Myers Briggs Type Indicator (MBTI) Workshops. Some of these are 'Basic' or 'Foundation' workshops, where the general theory is explained and people are encouraged to explore the concepts and 'discover' their own 'type', and to discuss this with others who are also engaged in a similar process of discovery. Other workshops are more specialized, and deal with issues relating to team building, or personal relationships, or educational issues. We have tried to cover these aspects in the first two parts of the book.

We both first came across MBTI within the broad educational programmes of the church, and we have used it extensively since then in church-based workshops, exploring some of the dimensions of faith. The third part of the book looks at how the church as an institution, and its patterns of leadership and activities, can be illuminated by a knowledge and understanding of type, and also how this knowledge and understanding can help us to explore and experience different kinds of spirituality and prayer.

This book comes from within the Christian tradition, and we

® MBTI and Myers Briggs Type Indicator are registered trademarks of Consulting Psychologists Press, Inc.

believe that part of that tradition is an emphasis on the possibilities of personal growth towards wholeness – which includes a recognition of both our strengths and weaknesses – as we journey towards a greater awareness of the reality and presence of God. It is a tradition which stresses the fact that, although we are born and die as individuals, we nevertheless live and move and have our being within communities, and that we need the insights and gifts and strengths of others to complement our own. For, as that most famous Dean of St Paul's Cathedral John Donne has reminded generations of people over the centuries, 'No man is an island, entire unto himself'.

We have written this book in such a way as to remain of interest to those who do not necessarily share our own beliefs. But for those who want to go on and explore how the MBTI can help them in their spiritual journey, we have made space, in Part Three, for that exploration to begin. There is more work to be done here but we did not think that an introductory text such as this, designed for a wide readership, was the right place.

We are conscious of the fact that virtually everything we have written is dependent upon the work and insight of others: upon those who have studied earlier, and written up their work, those who have led workshops and shared their experiences, knowledge and handouts with us, and upon those who have attended our own workshops, and by their comments and observations have enlarged our own understanding. We have tried to acknowledge sources of information and insight, but inevitably we have been unable to track down or inadvertently have omitted where some of our notes, stories or insights came from. There is a kind of mutually supporting informal network of practitioners; we have benefitted greatly from it, and we hope that what we have written may be of help to all those involved, in their own work.

In Britain, the Oxford Psychologists Press (OPP) acts as distributor for MBTI material, and it runs a number of excellent courses and is also responsible for training men and women to qualify for administering the Indicator. Based at Elsfield Hall, 15–17 Elsfield Way, Oxford OX2 8EP, it is the principal contact for material and information relating to the instrument. The overall publisher is the Consulting Psychologists Press Inc. in Palo Alto, California, and those who know the story of Isabel Briggs Myers will know of the important contribution that CPP made to the development and popularizing of her work.

We have referred a number of times to *The Type Reporter* which is an American monthly magazine publishing popular articles on personality type and temperament illustrating some of the many areas where they can be of interest and value. This can be ordered from 11314 Chapel Road, Fairfax Station, Virginia 22039, USA.

The basic authority on MBTI is by Isabel Briggs Myers and her son Peter. *Gifts Differing* is a very readable and important book for anyone wishing to know more about the Indicator. *Type Talk* by Otto Kroeger and Janet Thuesen, and *Please Understand Me* by David Keirsey and Marilyn Bates are probably the two most popular books on the subject, and we refer to them occasionally. In Part Three we acknowledge the work of Chester P Michael and Marie C Norrisey in *Prayer and Temperament*, and of Roy M Oswald and Otto Kroeger in *Personality Type and Religious Leadership*.

Few of the good things in life just 'happen to be': invariably there is a story to be told, and more than often there are one or two people whose vision, work and dedication have brought things to fruition. In our workshops we always spend some time explaining that behind the Myers Briggs Type Indicator there is the story of two remarkable women. It was inevitable therefore that we should want to pay tribute to them in our final chapter. The book *Katharine and Isabel: Mother's Light, Daughter's Journey* by Frances Wright Saunders, published by the CPP in 1995, gives a moving account of their remarkable lives.

Equally, we are both delighted and honoured that Peter Briggs Myers has written the Foreword to this book.

Malcolm Goldsmith
Martin Wharton

Part One

1 Vive La Différence!

Henry Higgins, in a song in the musical *My Fair Lady*, bemoans the fact that he finds it difficult to understand Eliza Doolittle; he attributes the problem to the fact that she is a woman, and asks: 'Why can't a woman be more like a man?' On further reflection, he recognizes that there might still be difficulties, and decides that the basic question should be: 'Why can't a woman, be more like *me*?'

There are obvious differences between men and women, but there are also obvious differences between some women and other women, and between some men and other men. Sometimes these differences lead to all sorts of problems, but sometimes they are seen and experienced as being extremely enriching. Coming to terms with the differences between people, with the vast array of different personality types, with different patterns of expression and different predilections for action, is both fascinating and frustrating, and many attempts have been made to increase our understanding and make the process easier.

Categorizing people is part and parcel of modern living. We are classified and categorized many times over each day of our lives. Our social class, our credit-worthiness, our qualifications – we are processed by a myriad of computer numbers which refer to our National Health number and National Insurance number, our bank statements, credit cards and driving licence, and so on. There is also a process of unconscious, or certainly less scientific, classification taking place. Our accent, our style of dress, our occupation or where we live all serve to place us in one sort of category or another. We may be aware of this or totally unaware of it, we may be irritated by it or sublimely indifferent to it; and the classifications may be accurate, reliable and useful or they may be nonsense. Whatever the case, we are summed up, classified, categorized or pigeon-holed, and we also make similar judgements about others.

As we look around at the people we know, we can see that they possess a variety of gifts and skills. No one person has all the gifts, and people react to each other and to situations in a variety of ways. Even so, we often feel that some people have everything

7

going for them. They seem to be endowed with every virtue and ability, whilst others (and we often include ourselves in this group) seem to be rather second-rate. And yet we know, from our own experience, that some of the most skilled people can be extremely difficult to get on with, and that some of those who appear at first sight to be less gifted, may have qualities which take us completely by surprise. Several years ago my mother had to go into hospital for an operation which would involve removing her nose; she was obviously totally dependent upon the skill of the surgeon, but it was a student nurse in her first week on the ward who sat up with her through the night and gave her strength and courage. In the process of healing, both the knowledge, judgement and skill of the doctors, and the compassion and availability of the nurse were needed. Each had something specific but different to offer, and neither could replace the other.

It is relatively easy to see and recognize different gifts when we look at the work that people do. Also, we can appreciate how important it is that there is a mixture of skills, aptitudes and methods of work available to us within the community. Football teams need the dependable solidity of one or two defenders, but they also need the mercurial talents of individual strikers if they are to challenge for the highest honours – it is often a painful experience for the supporter when injury to one player in a team means that other players have to adjust their play and take up positions that they are unfamiliar with and unsuited to.

Much the same sort of thing applies to human personality: we are all different, and none of us has all the gifts and none of us is entirely self-sufficient. Instead, each one of us is a mixture. There are some activities or tasks which come more easily to us than to others, there are certain situations in which we feel more at ease than others, and we have all developed particular ways of taking in information, sorting it out and acting upon it.

Over the years there have been many attempts to formulate theories and devise categories to help us make sense of these personality differences. The Myers Briggs Type Indicator® is one of these, and the aim of this book is to explain how it works, and to show what it can offer to us, in understanding our own

---

® MBTI and Myers Briggs Type Indicator are registered trademarks of Consulting Psychologists Press, Inc.

personality and preferences and also in understanding other people's. The name 'Myers Briggs' comes from the surnames of the two people who devised the Type Indicator, and who spent many many years working on their ideas and testing them out in a range of different situations. The final chapter in this book pays tribute to Isabel Briggs Myers (1897–1980) and her mother Katharine Cook Briggs (1875–1968), who were pioneers and workers of the highest calibre. They devoted their lives to finding a way of appreciating the differing gifts of people and to devising a framework which could help others to understand the strengths and weaknesses of different aspects of their personalities. 'Type Indicator' is the name given to this framework, hence the overall name of Myers Briggs Type Indicator, or MBTI for short.

Isabel Briggs Myers wrote her book *Gifts Differing*[1] shortly before she died, and dedicated it 'To all who desire to make fuller use of their gifts', and this affirmation of people lies at the heart of the whole process. If we can understand *how* and *why* we behave in the ways that we do, and why other people may act differently, then we have the chance of forming better relations with them, whether within the family or at work or in other social groups. If we can understand more about our own gifts and strengths, then we might be helped in finding a career or pastime which is more rewarding to us. Gaining insight into differing personality types and needs may well shed new light on our religious beliefs, too, and on our styles and patterns of prayer. Furthermore, if we can begin to understand why we find certain situations or particular people difficult to handle, then there is at least a chance that we might be able to discover ways of dealing with such problems in more constructive and creative ways.

It is important to stress at the outset that the MBTI does not measure intelligence, learning, stress, illness, trauma, maturity, emotions, IQ, psychiatric disturbances or 'normalcy'! It is a very valuable tool in helping us to understand our own personality type, and that of others, and it can be used in a wide variety of ways and situations, several of which we shall be exploring later. It is essentially an indicator which anyone can use, though it is probably less reliable for people in their early teens and younger. During the last decade work has been done to develop the Indicator in relation to primary school children, but that will be largely outside the scope of this book although mention of it will be made in Chapter 8. In recent years the MBTI has quickly become one of the largest selling and most popular tools of self-awareness available.

Shortly before Isabel Briggs Myers died, on 8 May 1980, she said that she dreamed that long after she had gone, her work would go on helping people. This commitment to 'helping people', to affirming their gifts and encouraging them to explore how they could value the gifts of others, lies at the heart of the MBTI. During the Second World War she wanted to find a way in which people who were different might help rather than destroy one another. She also saw a great many people volunteering for work for which they were totally unsuited, thus intensifying their experience of frustration and alienation. She wanted people so to understand the theory of personality type that they might be able to choose work which would make the greatest use of their gifts. As her work progressed, she wanted people to be able to use the Type Indicator as a tool for improving communications and teamwork.

She believed that the differences between people are valuable and interesting, and that there is a truly *mutual usefulness of opposites*, so she wanted people to be able to see type as a dynamic way of thinking, and as a means of gaining greater control over their lives. With such a tool, she believed that parents might be able to bring up their children in ways which would help them to develop their unique gifts to the full, thus preventing the problems that occur when people are not allowed to 'be themselves' and are expected to behave and belong in ways which bear little reference to their own personality type.

Valuing the differences of others, and appreciating the gifts of oneself more or less sums up the purposes of MBTI. Such simple aims belie the vast amount of work which undergirds the construction of the Indicator, and the careful way in which it has been developed in order to provide us with a fascinating and challenging way of looking at our own personality and the personality of others.

There is still considerable controversy surrounding the idea of distinct personality *types*. Many people would accept the view that the MBTI is a helpful indicator in personality *testing*, but they would not be prepared to go so far as admitting that there are specific personality types. Isabel Briggs Myers had a difficult time getting the Indicator accepted within academic psychological circles in America, and there are still many who treat it with great suspicion. Someone recently wrote to us saying: 'I have not yet met a clinical psychologist or psychiatrist who does not dismiss it', and yet, despite widespread professional scepticism, its use and influence is spreading rapidly, making it the world's most commonly used personality indicator. We hope that this book will give some indication why.

2 | What's It All About?

The idea of choice or preference is central to the theory of the Myers Briggs Type Indicator (MBTI). Although we may be *able* to act or think in various ways, we actually *prefer* to act and think in particular ways, and over the years we have all developed certain patterns of behaviour based on these preferences. For example, few of us can actually remember what it is like not to be able to ride a bicycle; at some time in our life we actually learned how to do it, and since then we have ridden automatically, without giving it further thought. In other aspects of our lives, too, we have found ways of doing things, or thinking things through, and as these ways have served us well in the past, so, unconsciously, we continue to use them.

A good introduction to MBTI is to invite people to write their names on a piece of paper using the hand that they don't normally use for writing; if you are right-handed you should therefore write your name out using your left hand, and vice versa (try it now and see what happens). Most people find this quite a cumbersome process. When I try to write with my left hand I have to think about it quite hard, I tend to feel embarrassed, it is a real struggle requiring effort and energy, and the end result is usually quite crude. I prefer to use my right hand; I'm not sure why, but it has always been easier to use than my left. It is more effective and efficient, it is used more often, relied upon more and much better developed than my left hand. My preferred hand is much more effective, but I do use my other hand when I need to. All of us have the capacity to use both hands, but we prefer one, and because we rely upon that one it becomes better developed. My preference for my right hand seems innate. So it is with personality types. We seem to be born with preferences for how we take in information, how we reach conclusions and come to decisions, and whether we prefer the inner or the outer world.

Another simple exercise illustrates the point: if I were to ask a group of people to sit down and cross their arms, no matter how often they did it, they would invariably cross their arms in the same way – either right over left, or left over right. To do it the other way would require a conscious effort. MBTI theory suggests that we have developed a whole range of preferences in the course of our lives, and that our personality type can be recognized by the totality of our individual preferences, which we express in a thousand different ways each day.

These preferences are explored in the questionnaire people are invited to complete when they undertake the Indicator. One of the surprises is to discover that none of the questions has a right or wrong answer, for they are all related to *preference*. Thus one question may explore whether you like making lists of things which need to be tackled over the weekend, whilst another may ask whether you prefer the word 'make' to 'create'. The questions, in themselves, seem small and inconsequential, but the overall effect of asking people to express their preferences is quite amazing. You will gather from this book that it is not essential to have answered the questionnaire, and it is possible to come to conclusions about personality type without it, but anyone who really wants to explore the Myers Briggs process fully will, at some stage, want to complete one of the questionnaires and take part in a workshop.

People's behaviour often seems to be random, but in fact it follows patterns, and these patterns are very basic. Thus, apparently random behaviour on an individual's part isn't random at all, and the patterns that we can detect reflect an individual's preferences for taking in information and for making decisions. They also reflect the world in which an individual feels most at home – the outer world of action, or the inner world of ideas. Once we become aware, and know what to look for, we will see that human behaviour is orderly and consistent over time.

One of the first people to explore the nature of such patterns of behaviour was the Swiss physician and psychologist Carl Jung. In his book *Psychological Types* (1923) he reflected on over twenty years' practice, and devised a way of separating out differing functions and processes of behaviour. It was the publication of this book which made such an impact upon Katharine Briggs and her daughter, and provided them with a theoretical framework which explained and complemented the work which they had been engaged in for many years. They took Jung's theories about Extraversion and Introversion, and about the mental processes of Perception and Judgement, and developed them. What we have today is a solid theoretical base, which is grounded in the work of

Jung but which has been developed and expanded. It is that framework which we are now about to explore.

An overview

According to Briggs and Myers there are sixteen different personality types; they are equally valid and each has its own particular strengths. No one type is more important or better than another. These sixteen types emerge by discovering where people fit on four distinct and separate scales, as a result of stating their preferences. It is important to recognize that *people place themselves*, and that the personality type which eventually emerges is the one that seems to 'fit' the individual. There is no secret or sinister 'system' which reveals what people do not want to know or which classifies people against their will. The Type Indicator almost always reveals what people already know about them-selves, but in a way which is structured and which enables them to understand and use the information creatively.

A step-by-step approach to the theory

1. Our behaviour is the result of how we receive information about the world (Perception) and how we reach decisions based on that information (Judgement). Naturally, we do both:

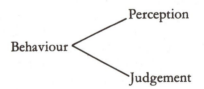

2. When it comes to taking in information (Perception), we make another choice. Some of us choose to rely upon our five senses (touch, taste, sight, hearing, smell). We know something about the world in which we live because we have experienced it directly through our senses and we trust the data. Others of us, however, prefer to take in information through what amounts to our sixth sense, which is our intuition, hunches, or gut feelings. We prefer to see things as they could possibly be rather than as they actually are. Each of us prefers to take in

information either through 'Sensing' or through 'iNtuition'. Of course, we all use both Sensing and iNtuition, but we trust and rely on one more than on the other – we prefer it:

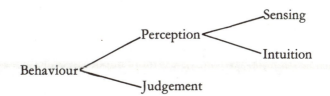

3. Just as there is a preference for how we take in information, so there is also a preference for how we come to conclusions, make decisions and arrive at judgements. Some of us will prefer our 'Thinking' function – we will decide things in an impersonal way based on analysis and principles, and a premium will be placed upon fairness. Others of us, however, have a preference for Feeling: we tend to make decisions and judgements based upon our likes and dislikes, upon our own personal system of values and on the impact that the decisions will have upon other people. Those who prefer 'Feeling' to 'Thinking' will place a premium upon harmony:

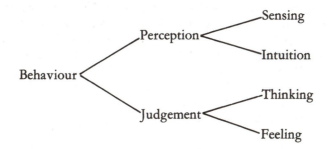

4. The final part of the theory tells us where we prefer to go to receive personal energy. Some of us prefer to find our energy in the world of people and things outside ourselves. Extraverts are drawn to the external world and the relationships which they enjoy there, and spend less time with their thoughts and concepts. Others of us, however, find our energy in the inner world of ideas and concepts. We have a preference for the inner world and consequently require less of the outside world:

15

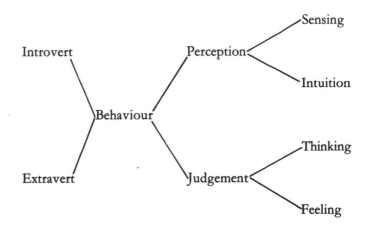

5. The four sets of preferences are thus:

Extraversion	*or*	Introversion
Sensing	*or*	Intuition
Thinking	*or*	Feeling
Judgement	*or*	Perception

For obvious reasons these essential eight words are abbreviated down to letters, and so we have **E**xtravert and **I**ntrovert, **S**ensing and i**N**tuition, **T**hinking and **F**eeling, and **J**udgement and **P**erception. As a result of answering the questionnaire each person finishes up with four letters which indicate their personality type. They will be *either* E or I, *either* S or N, *either* T or F, and *either* J or P. The two writers of this book are ENFJ and ENTP – you will appreciate later on how we would very much have liked one of us to have been an S!

Extravert or Introvert?

Everyone, at certain times and in certain situations, can be either Extravert or Introvert; that is, we are all capable of operating in that particular 'mode'. What we are wanting to discover is how people *prefer* to operate, and we are wanting to discover the person in their 'relaxed', 'slipper-wearing', 'off-duty' mood. Our daily work often makes considerable demands upon us to operate in a certain way, we recognize this, but in seeking to establish a person's basic personality type we want him/her to forget, as far

16

as possible, the pressures of work – indeed, to forget all other sorts of pressures, to relax and *be him/herself!*.

Extraversion and Introversion are complementary attitudes towards the world. An Extravert's essential stimulation comes from the outer world of people and things – they are what energizes him or her, whilst an Introvert's essential stimulation comes from within, from his or her inner world of reflections and thoughts.

Put another way, we can say that the Extravert feels pulled out and stimulated by external claims and situations, whereas the Introvert may well feel daunted by them and pulled inward. The Extravert is energized and set alight by other people and a whole range of external experiences, whereas the Introvert gains his or her energy from inner resources and internal reflections and experiences. The Extravert seeks stimulation in the outer world or environment; the Introvert seeks it in their inner world or environment.

We can use a process of word association to contrast the two, and here are just a few examples:

Extraverts	Introverts
Active	Reflective
People	Solitude
Noise	Quiet
Sociable	Reserved
Many	Few
Breadth	Depth

Extraverts are often friendly, talkative and easy to get to know; they express their emotions and blossom in relationships. They give breadth to life and are outgoing. Introverts, on the other hand, are often more reserved, and they take longer to get to know; they may hide their emotions and need space. They give depth to life and are more private.

Introverts often experience Extraverts as being shallow, whilst Extraverts may experience Introverts as being withdrawn.

Let us now transfer these types into a work situation and begin to compare how they operate (see chart below).

Extravert types	Introvert types
Like variety and action	Like quiet for concentration
Direct their attention mostly to the outer world of people and things	Direct their attention mostly to the inner world of ideas
Tend to be faster and impatient with complicated details	Tend to be careful with details and dislike sweeping statements
Are often good at greeting people	May have trouble remembering names and faces
Often dislike long slow jobs	Don't mind working on one job for a long time
Don't mind the telephone	Often dislike the telephone and its interruptions
Like to have people around	Are content to work alone
Can be drained or bored if required to spend too much time alone	Can find too much time with people, especially strangers, draining
Speak out easily and often at meetings	Tend to hold back at meetings and may have trouble getting into the discussion
May dislike and avoid writing	Often have good writing skills and may prefer to present ideas in writing
Are relatively easy to get to know	Take longer to get to know
Regard action above thought	Can be so deep in thought that they fail to act

Put another way:

If you are an Extravert, you probably . . .

● tend to talk first and think later
● don't know what you are going to say until you hear yourself saying it
● know lots of people and include as many as you can in your activities
● don't mind having conversations with the radio or television on in the background – you may be oblivious to this kind of distraction
● are approachable and easily engaged by friends and strangers
● find telephone calls a welcome interruption, and don't mind making calls when you have something to tell someone
● prefer generating ideas within groups rather than by yourself
● 'look' with your mouth rather than with your eyes – thus you might well say 'I've lost my pen, has anyone seen it?'
● need affirmation from your friends about who you are, what you do and how you look. You may think that your work has been well done but until you hear someone tell you, you don't really believe it

If you are an Introvert, you probably . . .

● rehearse things before saying them, and prefer others to do the same
● enjoy the peace and quiet of having time to yourself
● are thought to be a good listener
● have been thought of as reserved or shy – whether or not you agree
● like to share special occasions with just one or two close friends
● wish you could get some of your ideas out more clearly, and sometimes resent those who blurt out things that you are just about to say
● like stating your thoughts or feelings without interruption
● need to 'recharge' alone when you have spent time with a larger group

Extraverts use both their E (Extraversion) and I (Introversion), but prefer E. Introverts use both E (Extraversion) and I (Introversion), but prefer I. No one is 100 per cent introvert or 100 per cent extravert, but we do all have a preference for one rather than the other. The MBTI questionnaire helps us to assess the clarity and strength of our preference.

For Carl Jung the distinction between Extraversion and Introversion is the most important one between people, because it describes the source, direction and focus of their energy. Consequently, whether at home, at work or at school, the extent to which we are able to resort to the preferred source of our energy will have a significant effect upon the quality of our daily lives.

Sensing or Intuition?

The Extraversion–Introversion (E-I) scale is about where people like to focus their attention and whether they are energized by the inner or outer world. The Sensing – iNtuition (S–N) scale is about how people receive information. The Sensing function takes in information by way of our senses – sight, sound, smell, taste and touch, whilst the iNtuiting function gains information by way of a 'sixth sense' or hunch. They are two essential ways of perceiving the world. Sensing types or Sensers attend to specifics which come to them through their senses and they are aware of the specifics and facts of their present experience; intuitive types or iNtuitives attend to the patterns and meanings which come to them via their imagination or memory and they are aware of possibilities and imaginings by way of their insight. All of us use both functions, but we *prefer* one to the other. The one we prefer, like our 'right' hand, will be much more developed than the other.

Sensers tend to look at specific parts and pieces whereas iNtuitives look at patterns and relationships. Sensers live in the present, enjoying what is there; iNtuitives live for the future, imagining and anticipating what might be ahead. INtuitives prefer imagining possibilities; Sensers prefer handling present practicalities.

Using word association for this pair (Sensers and iNtuitives) we find words such as:

Sensers	Intuitives
Details	Patterns
Facts	Ideas
Present	Future
Repetition	Variety
Directions	Hunches
Practical	Imaginative

Sensers like things that are measurable, definite, concrete; they like to start at the beginning and take one step at a time, they like set procedures and clear directions. All this contrasts quite markedly with iNtuitives who like opportunities to be inventive; they tend to jump in anywhere and get bored with details – they seldom read instructions! INtuitives like change and variety and are always looking at what might be; they see the whole wood rather than individual trees, whereas Sensers often don't see the wood at all, because their attention is focused upon individual trees.

We recently saw some information about a job. The details of the accommodation which went with the post were described in the following way: 'A light, spacious and well-decorated apartment with magnificent views down to the Firth of Forth and across to Fife' – no further details were given, no mention of how many rooms, heating facilities and so on. In fact, there were no details of any kind, it was a classic piece of writing by an iNtuitive type!

Sensers may seem to be unduly materialistic and literal to many iNtuitives, whilst to Sensers, iNtuitives may seem to be impractical daydreamers who are impossible to pin down.

Let us now transfer these types into a work situation and see if we can begin to identify certain characteristics:

Sensing types	Intuitive types
Dislike new problems unless there are standard ways of solving them	Like solving new problems
Like established routines	Dislike routines
Tend to be good at precise work	Dislike taking time for precision
Mostly work all the way through to reach a conclusion	Often jump to conclusions
See 'what is'	See 'what could be'
Seldom make errors of fact	Often make errors of fact
Often like absorbing facts for their own sake	Easily get bored with facts
Are quick to grasp details	Tend to disregard the details
Enjoy using skills already learned rather than acquiring new ones	Enjoy learning a new skill more than using it
Are over-reliant on history, tradition and established procedures	Tend to ignore the lessons of history
See the objections to new ideas before the good points	Easily overlook practical problems which may come with new ideas
Are specific and literal when speaking or writing	Are general and abstract when speaking or writing

If you are a Senser, then you probably . . .

● prefer specific answers to specific questions
● like to concentrate on what you are doing at the moment, and don't think ahead
● prefer to do something, rather than think about it
● find most satisfying those jobs which lead to a tangible result
● believe that 'if something isn't broken, you don't have to mend it'! You don't understand why some people have to try and improve everything
● would rather work with facts and figures than with theories and ideas
● get frustrated when people don't give you clear instructions
● are literal in your use of words, and take things literally
● subscribe to the notion that 'seeing is believing'; if someone tells you that the bus is here, you won't really believe it until you are on board!

If you are an iNtuitive, you will probably . . .

● tend to think about several things at once, and sometimes be accused of being absent-minded
● find the future and its possibilities more intriguing and fascinating than frightening and worrying
● be more excited about where you are going than where you are
● believe that time is relative, and that you are not late until the meeting/meal/party has started without you
● find yourself looking for the connection between things or events, rather than taking them at their face value
● find yourself asking 'Why?'
● tend to give general answers to most questions and get irritated when you are pushed for specifics
● dream about how to spend your next salary increase rather than sit and balance your bank account

If you were to ask a person 'How was your day today?', Sensing types will tend to give you a detailed account of how their time was spent – for example, 'at 9a.m. I met with the staff for our weekly meeting, then at 11a.m. I went on a visit to . . .'; iNtuitive types, on the other hand, will tend to give you a much more general, conceptual answer – for example, 'it was a bit tricky, I had to sort out the staffing issues . . .'.

Remember, iNtuitives look for the meaning of an event or an experience, whereas Sensers tend to examine its various components. Sensers like to understand a process by looking at it sequentially, whereas iNtuitives randomly gather information and fit it into a theoretical model. For iNtuitive types everything is relational and must have meaning. If an iNtuitive person isn't looking for something in particular he or she may well walk right past it, never even noticing its existence. Sensing types tend to find this characteristic difficult to understand, for them something is there, it is real, it exists, and it is difficult to fathom how people cannot, or do not, see it.

A conversation between a Senser (S) and an iNtuitive (N) might well go like this:

S: What time is it?
N: It's late.
S: (surprised) What time is it?
N: It's time to go.
S: (impatient) What time is it?
N: Why are you asking?.
S: WHAT TIME IS IT?!!!
N: It's just after three!

Sensers want specific answers to their specific questions, whereas iNtuitives may find lots of ways to reply, none of which may be satisfactory to the Senser questioner.

In the work situation, Sensing types may see iNtuitive types as being rather slapdash, lacking in concentration and living with their heads in the clouds. Conversely, the iNtuitives might well see the Sensers as being slow, plodding, head-down and blinkered!

The truth is, that we are all part Senser and part iNtuitive; what we need to know is what our *preference* is, and how well we have developed that preference.

Thinking or Feeling?

We come now to the third of our dimensions. Thinking and Feeling are two essential ways of making rational judgements, of coming to decisions about the information we have perceived through either our senses or our intuition. The Thinking function decides on the basis of objective considerations and logic, whereas the Feeling function decides on the basis of subjective, personal values. Once again, we all use both methods, but we *prefer* one to the other.

There are probably more misunderstandings associated with this choice than with any of the others, so it needs to be clearly grasped that we are *not* saying that a person who operates via the Thinking process has no feelings, nor that the person who operates via the Feeling process has no brain – in fact we have a great friend who is a Professor who is clearly and unambiguously a 'Feeler.' You can have a first class honours degree and be a Feeler; you can be of rather average intelligence and be a Thinker. The words used by Myers Briggs are not intended to be descriptive of a person's intelligence or emotions.

Thinkers make decisions by way of logical analysis, they use objective and impersonal criteria and seek rational order by logic. Feelers make their decisions by way of person-centred values, they seek rational order through harmony and place considerable weight on human values and motives. It is almost a truism to say that Thinkers decide with their heads whereas Feelers decide with their hearts: the Feeler will go by personal convictions rather than by logic and will have a greater concern for relationship and harmony than the Thinker who will be more concerned for truth and justice.

In terms of word association for Thinkers and Feelers, we could expect the following to appear quite often:

Thinkers	Feelers
Head	Heart
Objective	Subjective
Justice	Harmony
Precise	Persuasive
Principles	Values
Cool	Caring
Impersonal	Personal

25

The Thinker will tend to see things from the outside, as an observer, whilst the Feeler will be more inclined to be identified with what is going on and view things as a participant. The Thinker will tend to take a cool, long look at things, whereas the Feeler will tend to be more immediate and take a personal view. The Thinker will be inclined to be spontaneously evaluative, whereas the Feeler's immediate response is to be appreciative.

Thinkers may seem to be cold and perhaps rather condescending to Feelers, whereas Feelers may seem to be emotional and muddled to Thinkers.

Placing the types in a work situation, we are likely to witness the following:

Thinking types	Feeling types
Relatively unemotional and uninterested in people's feelings	Tend to be very aware of other people and their feelings
May hurt people's feelings without knowing it	Enjoy pleasing people, even in small things
May seem to be hard-hearted	Tend to be sympathetic
Set out their communications in a logical order	Set out their communications by identifying with the recipient
Can get along without harmony	Like and need harmony
Need to be treated fairly	Need occasional praise
Dislike or ignore the irrational components of human behaviour	Understand and take into account the irrational
Settle disputes by appeal to objective criteria	Settle disputes by appeal to human values and harmony
Tend to make their decisions impersonally, sometimes ignoring people's wishes and feelings	Often let their decisions be influenced by their own or other people's wishes and feelings

Can be ruthless	Can be easily hurt
May fail to convince other people through thinking that pure logic will win the argument, and fail to identify with the listener	May strive for harmony to the point where necessary tough decisions are postponed, which may mean that the situation gets worse
When situations call for it, able to reprimand people, or sack them	When situations call for it have difficulty telling people unpleasant things
Good at exploring the logical, impersonal consequences of actions or decisions	Good at assessing the human consequences of actions or of decisions

Once again, it is important to stress that we are *not* saying that Thinkers cannot get hurt, or that they do not want harmony. Similarly, we are *not* saying that Feelers do not think or are not logical. It is important to emphasize that we all operate in both modes, but we have a *preference* for one rather than the other.

So, if you are a Thinker, you probably . . .

- stay cool, calm, collected and objective in situations where others are upset
- prefer to settle a dispute based on what is fair and truthful rather than on what will make people happy
- enjoy proving a point, for the sake of clarity – and you will sometimes argue both sides in a discussion to provoke and stretch the thinking of others
- tend to be more firm-minded than tender-hearted (if you disagree with people you will prefer to tell them rather than say nothing)
- value your objectivity despite the fact that some people may regard you as uncaring (you know this is untrue)
- don't mind making difficult decisions and think it is more important to be right than to be liked
- are impressed with things that are logical and scientific – and until you receive some more information, you are probably sceptical about MBTI!

27

If, on the other hand, you are a Feeler, you will probably . . .

- consider that a good decision is one that takes people's feelings into account
- over-extend yourself in meeting other people's needs. You will do almost anything to help others, maybe at the expense of your own comfort and needs
- put yourself into 'other people's shoes' and feel where they are 'pinching' (in a meeting you are likely to ask: 'How will this affect the people involved?')
- enjoy providing services for other people, even if you are sometimes exploited
- find yourself wondering, 'Doesn't anyone care about what *I* want?', though you would probably never admit this to anyone!
- not hesitate to take back something you've said if it has caused offence: you are sometimes accused of being 'wishy-washy'
- prefer harmony to clarity: you don't like conflict and will tend to avoid it: 'Let's change the subject', or: 'Let's kiss and make up'
- be accused of taking things too personally

Remember, we are talking about the process the individual *prefers* in making a decision. Each of us prefers to make decisions either through a process of objective impersonal analysis or through our subjective system of values.

Judgement or Perception?

We come now to the fourth pair of 'letters'. Extraversion and Introversion (E and I) deals with the world in which we prefer to focus our attention and receive our energy; Sensing (S) and iNtuition (N) deals with how we take in and receive information; Thinking and Feeling, (T and F), deals with how we make decisions about that information, and now, with Judgement and Perception (J and P) we deal with how we relate towards the outer world, how we deal with the external environment.

Once again it is important to sound a note of caution, the words which are used here: Judgement and Perception, should not be confused with the everyday meanings of the commonly-used words Judgemental and Perceptive. In Myers Briggs terminology a Judging lifestyle is one which is decisive, planned and orderly, whereas a Perceptive lifestyle is one which is flexible, adaptable and spontaneous. Both are of equal value and neither carries with it any negative connotations. Everyone is capable of operating in both modes, and indeed, we all do so at some time or another, but we all actually *prefer* one to the other.

Judgers prefer an organized lifestyle: they like structure and order and like to have things under control: Perceivers on the other hand, prefer a more flexible approach. They tend to experience life as it happens and to go along with the current. Judgers like to be decisive and to know what the boundaries are to any situation; Perceivers enjoy being spontaneous and like to have freedom to explore, to change their minds and to keep as many options open as possible. Judgers are always moving towards closure; Perceivers are always trying to keep things open. For Judgers, *today* is the important issue; for Perceivers, *tomorrow* might well bring something better. Judgers are liable to make decisions too early and Perceivers are liable to miss out on making decisions at all.

Words which might be associated with Judgers and Perceivers would include:

Judgers	Perceivers
Organized	Flexible
Decisive	Wait and see
Planned	Spontaneous
Pre-arranged	Open-ended
Closure	Openness
Deadlines	Discoveries
Control	Adaptation

Judgers handle deadlines well, and like to plan in advance; Perceivers tend to meet deadlines in a last-minute rush. It is sometimes said that you can distinguish a J from a P by looking at the inside of their cars – one will have old newspapers, gloves, scarves, de-icer cans and a multitude of filling-station receipts all over the place, whilst the other will be clean and tidy, with maps carefully placed in the pockets and a torch handy (just in case!).

Judgers may seem to be too demanding, rigid, inflexible and uptight to Perceivers, whilst Perceivers may seem to be downright disorganized, messy and even irresponsible to Judgers.

Once again we can use the work situation to illustrate facets of behaviour that point out the differences:

Judging types	Perceiving types
Dislike interrupting one task for another; work according to a schedule	Start many projects, have difficulty finishing them, and postpone unpleasant tasks
Want authority, structure and predictability	Want autonomy, variety and stimulation
Aim to be right, and to master something	Aim to miss nothing and to try everything
Like to get things settled and tied up	Don't mind leaving things open for last minute alterations
Tend to be rated as effective managers	Tend to be rated as creative professionals
Live according to plans, customs and objectives, to which events must conform	Live according to the moment and adjust easily to the unexpected
Are best when they can plan their work and stick to the plan	Tend to be good at adapting to changing situations
May be slow to see the need for change and may be reluctant to adapt plans	May get bored easily and seek change for change's sake
Can be satisfied once they reach a decision	Remain curious and welcome new light even when a decision has been reached

Tend to be reluctant to move from, or question given values	Have difficulty making decisions and sticking to them
Come to conclusions too quickly and ignore evidence to the contrary	Seldom come to a decision because there is always more information to consider
Tend to be comfortable in hierarchical organizations which have authority, structure and predictability	Tend to be resistant to authority, which can lead to under-performance in hierarchical organizations

If you are a Judging type you probably . . .

- always seem to be waiting for others who never seem to be on time
- have a place for everything and are not satisfied until everything is in the right place
- 'know' that if everyone did what they were supposed to do, then the world would be a better place
- know each morning more or less what your day is going to be like – it will be planned and you will follow the plan. You may be annoyed or disorientated if it doesn't turn out as expected
- are not keen on surprises of any kind (and people know)
- keep lists and use them. If you do something not on your list you may add it to your list so that you can cross it off!
- like to work things through to their conclusion and completion and get them off your desk, even if you know that you might have to do them again later to get them right

If you are a Perceiving type you probably . . .

- get distracted easily – you can 'get lost' going upstairs!
- love to explore the unknown, even if it is something as small as a new route from home to work
- don't plan a task, but wait to see what it demands
- get accused by others of being disorganized (but you know better)
- have to depend upon last minute spurts of energy to meet deadlines, and you may drive everyone crazy in the process!

31

- don't believe that neatness is especially important, even though you might lose things: the important things are creativity, spontaneity and responsiveness
- turn most work into play – if it can't be fun then it's probably not worth doing
- often change the subject in conversations – and the new topic can be anything that enters your head, or the room
- don't like to be pinned down about things (anyway, you might not even be a 'P'!)
- tend, often, to make things less than definite, from time to time, but not always, it all depends!

In other words, if you are a Judger you can plan your work and work your plan. Even your leisure time is structured and organized. There is usually a right and a wrong way to do everything, from applying for a job to stacking plates in the washing-up rack. If, however, you are a Perceiver, you will prefer a 'wait and see' attitude on most things, whether it is on what work needs to be done or how to solve a particular problem. Perceivers tend to perceive, not to draw conclusions or come to decisions. Judgers on the other hand, tend to make decisions rather than to respond to new information, even if that information might change the decision. At the extremes Ps find it virtually impossible to make a decision and Js find it almost impossible to change theirs!

The Judgement–Perception preference is probably the most significant source of tension in interpersonal relationships. Judgers can irritate Perceivers with their continuing need for closure and having a plan and schedule for everything. Perceivers can irritate Judgers with their ability to be spontaneous and easy-going about everything. Remember, neither is right or wrong, or more or less desirable: we *need* both types, and we can all operate in both modes, but we *prefer* one to the other.

Settling on a preference type

We have now looked at the four dimensions which, when placed in conjunction with each other, make up the Type Indicator. Every person will have a preference for either E or I, either S or N, either T or F and either J or P. Taking the four letters that make up his/her preferences, a person will arrive at one of sixteen different combinations of letters, and those letters will indicate his/her personality type. In our next chapter we give expanded accounts of how these combinations act together to produce recognizable personality types. The letters are put together in the following arrangement:

ISTJ	ISFJ	INFJ	INTJ
ISTP	ISFP	INFP	INTP
ESTP	ESFP	ENFP	ENTP
ESTJ	ESFJ	ENFJ	ENTJ

Anyone wanting to explore the Type Indicator in any detail should familiarize themselves with the table above. You will see that there is a definite pattern to the placing of the letters, and they always appear in the same order. There is a theoretical reason for this but it need not detain us now. The diagrams below show how the Type Table is broken down.

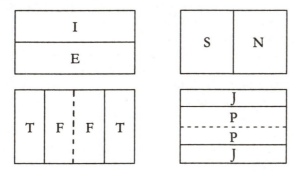

Identifying the dominant

Imagine that four people are all speaking at the same time, they are speaking about the same thing, perhaps they are describing a film which they have seen recently. They are all using different words as they describe the film from their own perspective. This may be a difficult scenario to visualize. But now imagine that one person is speaking in the quietest of whispers, another is talking fairly quietly but certainly not in a whisper, the third has a naturally loud voice and it is being used to good effect, and the last person is positively yelling. It would be difficult to hear what any of them was saying, but in the end we would hear the loudest and perhaps be totally oblivious of the whispered contribution.

A similar sort of process is taking place within us! Our processes of perception (Sensing and iNtuition) and judgement (Thinking and Feeling) are all operating all of the time – rather like the four voices in our example. We are constantly taking in information, processing it and deciding what to do with it. The letters of our personality type now give us a basis for exploring further what our 'dominant process' (the 'loudest voice') is. By 'dominant process' we mean that function which is the driving force of our personality, the 'captain of the ship' as it were.

We find in our workshops that the dominant process is often the most difficult part of the theory for people to grasp, although once it has 'clicked' it is simple enough to follow and to use, and so we will spell it out step by step:

Locating the dominant process

1. The dominant process will be found within the central letters, the 'functions' of our personality type profile. It will be either S or N, or T or F. [Because I am an ENTP this means that my dominant will be either N or T. If I were an ISFJ my dominant would be either S or F.]
2. The outer letters, E and I, J and P, are involved and act as indicators.
3. The final letter, J or P, indicates whether the dominant is likely to be in the judging function (T or F) or in the perceiving function (S or N). So, J at the end of our type profile points to either T or F (whichever we have) and P points to either S or N. *We should now be focusing on just one letter.* [Because I am an ENTP that letter, for me, is N; if I were an ISFJ that letter would be F.]
4. The letter we have now focused on (as in 3. above) signifies what we show to the outside world, as opposed to what we retain for our inner world.
5. If the first letter in our type profile is E (Extravert), this means

that we tend to show the best of ourselves to the outside world, and therefore the process/letter which has emerged in 3. above is our dominant process. [Thus for me, an ENTP, my dominant is my iNtuition.]

6. However, if we are an Introvert, having an I as our first letter, then we don't show our best to the outer world but keep it for our inner world. So, as 3. above gave us the letter which signifies what we show to the outer world, then it follows that the other letter (in the middle two) is what we keep for our inner world – and for Introverts *that* is the dominant. [If I were an ISFJ my dominant would therefore be my Sensing function.]

Simple!

It is important for us to identify our dominant because, although we use all four functions – Sensing, iNtuition, Feeling and Thinking, we do not use them equally well. From our earliest days we will have developed the habit of using one more than the others. It will have seemed more trustworthy to us than the others, and as we used it more, so it became more developed and reliable. Thus, gradually it became the central process in our personality, around which all the others revolve.

The Type Table below now gives all 16 types again, but with the dominant functions highlighted (in bold):

IS**T**J	IS**F**J	IN**F**J	IN**T**J
IS**T**P	IS**F**P	IN**F**P	IN**T**P
ES**T**P	ES**F**P	E**N**FP	E**N**TP
ES**T**J	ES**F**J	EN**F**J	EN**T**J

Identifying the auxiliary

People are not one-dimensional with a dominant trait only. There is also an auxiliary function to support the dominant one. The auxiliary function is always formed in the dimension that the dominant is *not* in, and so it is the other letter in the central pair. Thus an ENTP will have N as the dominant and T as the auxiliary, and an ISFJ will have S as the dominant and F as the auxiliary, and so on. When these personality types are being discussed, these two – the dominant and the auxiliary – are often linked together, so we can speak of 'iNtuition with Thinking' or 'Sensing with Feeling'. In such couplings the dominant is always given first, and so if I say that I am an 'Extraverted iNtuitive with Thinking' (or an 'Introverted iNtuitive with Thinking') then it is clear that my dominant is iNtuition and my auxiliary is Thinking.

We have already noted that Introvert types do not show their best to the outside world but keep it for their inner world. What they do, therefore, show to the outer world is their auxiliary. It is important to remember this when meeting with Introvert types, and especially important when interviewing them. What is presented to the world – to you – is not the most developed, central function, it is the auxiliary function.

What we are seeking to achieve (and we will discuss this later) is the development of our other dimensions, so that we are not totally reliant upon our dominant. There are many situations in which it is more fitting to use other functions, and if these have not been recognized and developed, then we are likely to respond to situations or people in an inappropriate manner.

The value of the auxiliary is that it acts rather like a 'best friend' to the dominant, supporting it whilst at the same time challenging it. As an iNtuitive (N) with Thinking (T) my dominant is my iNtuition, which takes me off on many a flight of fancy, but because my auxiliary is Thinking there is a reasonable chance that most of my ideas will be harnessed by my T to see if they have some logical basis, and hopefully I am saved from my worst excesses! However, because my dominant is N, in the final analysis I may choose to follow my 'hunch' even though I recognize that all the parts do not necessarily hang together in a logical way.

As a games inventor, my iNtuition (N) is of enormous importance to me as I follow up ideas and endeavour to come up with creative game-play mechanisms and novel ideas which might be translated into a board or card game. Most of my hunches come to nothing (they wither away in the cool light of my T) but occasionally I persevere – even though my T tells me that the idea is stupid – and then, very occasionally, there is a break-through and my N is vindicated! Without my T, I would be inundated with ideas which lead nowhere; without my N, I would never dare to believe in my ideas.

The least preferred functions

In Jung's theory, the two kinds of perception are opposite to each other. Sensing and iNtuition are at the opposite ends of a single continuum. If we have identified which is our dominant function – that is, the process that we are most at home with, that we use most often and have developed most – then it follows that the opposite process is the one which is least preferred, used most infrequently, and with which we feel least at home. Therefore, for most of us, using that function is rather like writing with our left hand if we are right-handed. We feel clumsy, self-conscious and are none too happy with the result! We may find that using our least preferred function makes us quite tired and may cause us to make unforced errors. We therefore need to work on it, so that when occasions arise when this is the most appropriate function to use, we are able to proceed without undue difficulty.

Being a person with a strongly dominant N this means that my S is rather underdeveloped – a fact brought home to me only too forcibly recently. I applied to the Inland Revenue for tax relief on a mortgage that I was taking out and was informed that they would consider it when I completed my tax returns for the previous three years. No one likes completing income tax forms, but dominant Ns like doing it even less than others!

Just as our least preferred function is the opposite of our dominant, so our 'third preference' is the opposite to our auxiliary. Some people call these opposites to our dominant and auxiliary our 'shadow', but this term is not ideal as the word means something different in Jung's writing. Other people refer to them as our 'inferior' functions. The authors, here, prefer to stick to 'third and fourth preferences' or 'third preference' and 'least preferred'. Whatever name we give to them, they are nevertheless important, and in our journey to maturity we need to be able to handle and develop them. It is sometimes said that in later life, when we perhaps have more time and are less thrusting, we turn our attention more to these. It is certainly an interesting and worthwhile subject to reflect upon.

Sometimes our least preferred functions can be of use to people in helping them to understand or discern their personality type precisely because it is the one which gives them the most trouble and is the most difficult for them to handle. A dominant Thinker, for example, may be overcome by feeling and conclude that he or she is really the Feeling type; and a dominant Feeler might mistake himself or herself for a Thinker because he or she happens to be dominated or obsessed with one particular idea. It can happen that some people recognize their type most easily as a result of the sometimes humiliating or painful effects of their least preferred functions.

A few caveats

As we come to the end of this chapter, which has been primarily concerned with explaining the theory and structure of the Myers Briggs Type Indicator, there are just a few things that we need to watch out for. The first is to stress that *there are no 'good' or 'bad' types*: each type is different and has its own particular strengths. Of course, there may be good and bad people within each type, but that is another matter!

Personality type is dynamic, not static, which means that it is a process, it is changing and developing all the time. Jung believed that we were born with our own 'ideal type', but that it may take us a long time to discover it, because our background and training, our environment and the pressures that we live under can all serve to hide or skew our fundamental type. Added to this, is the fact that we do not always behave 'according to type' and we have the choice or possibility of using the most appropriate function in a specific situation, even if it is not our preferred function.

In the next chapter we will describe, in greater detail, each of the 16 types. We must remember that there are wide individual variations within each type. It has been said that we are like everyone else in our type, we are like some others in our type, and we are like no one else in our type. We have a Friends of the Earth postcard with a picture of a zebra drawn by Louise Beckerman, and surrounding the animal are the words 'No one zebra is striped exactly like another'.

People answering the MBTI questionnaire have numbers allotted to each of their preferences and these can be very helpful, but they can also be misleading if used incorrectly. It is essential to remember that the numbers indicate our strength of preference between the two ends of the continuum. They do *not* indicate high skill in a particular area. Thus, a person with, say, a high F score is not necessarily a sympathetic and caring sort of person, and a person with a low T score is not therefore someone who is not very good at thinking. The scores indicate a person's *preference*. It is also important to remember that one score cannot be compared with another – whether your own score on a different dimension or the score of someone else on the same dimension. A person who, let's say, scores 30 on their N and 12 on their F cannot then assume that their N is much stronger or better than their F; the scoring refers *only* to the scale on which it was measured. Nor can one person who scores 30 on their N assume that they are more creative than someone else who scores just 5 on their N; the scores refer only to the strength of preferences of the person concerned. One final point concerning the questionnaire scoring. There is no 'ideal distribution', we are not trying to get a specific cluster of scores, to be on the borderline between the two extremes, or anything else. The scores represent, as it were, a snapshot of our preferences. It is important that we understand what they mean and that we do not give them a significance which is not valid.

The questionnaire is copyrighted and we are not able to reproduce it, but you will probably have gathered from the earlier pages that it is not essential. It has the advantage of giving you numerical values to your preferences, and we would certainly encourage people to attend a Myers Briggs workshop and complete a questionnaire so that they will experience feedback and insight from a qualified professional. It is not, though, a prerequisite for the purpose of discovering your type, and working on that information.

The Myers Briggs Type Indicator is a self-report instrument, and it is therefore open to error. For instance, your mood when you complete the questionnaire, can affect the end result, and so can a host of other variables. Having said that, a great amount of work has been done to ensure the validity and reliability of the Indicator, and provided the questionnaire is completed with care and without stress or compulsion, then it is very likely that subsequent 're-takes' will come up with the same type formula, or with modification in just one of the four areas. In the end, you will know whether the type indicated 'fits' you; if it doesn't, then you will need to read around the descriptions of other types and give them further thought until you finally end up with what you believe to be the right description and type for you. In our experience the vast majority of people very quickly find a type formula which suits them.

3 Profiles of the Different Types

ISTJ
Introverted Sensing with Thinking

ISTJ types are realistic, dependable, practical people. They tend to be accurate and careful in the way they deal with the facts which their Sensing preference has gathered. Their focus on the present leads them not to take anything for granted and what they perceive is analysed and translated objectively (by their Thinking preference), which they then organize, structure and schedule. Since all of this comes naturally to them, they tend to expect it of everyone else and they can be demanding at home and at work.

ISTJs are driven by a sense of responsibility, which they accept willingly. Dependability is one of their qualities, the word of an ISTJ is their bond. They perform their duties without a flourish and the dedication they bring to their work can go unnoticed.

ISTJs are thorough, systematic, hard-working and careful with rules and precedents. They offer a stabilizing presence in organizations and often rise to positions of responsibility, which is seen by them as simply doing their duty – 'doing what *should* be done'; indeed 'should' is a key part of their make up.

If ISTJs are found in management or executive positions, their practical judgement and acceptance of established procedures makes them dependable, and consistent in approach. They will tend to seek solutions to current problems in the successes of the past.

ISTJs communicate a message of stability and reliability. They are pillars of strength in the home, at work and in their community organizations, but they may encounter problems if they expect everyone to be as logical and analytical as they are themselves.

In the home, they take their responsibilities to their children and partners very seriously. Parenting is seen as a life-long responsibility. They are loyal, faithful, dutiful, dependable and consistent to their partners and children. Rules and regulations will be imposed on their children in the expectation they will be followed. A rebellious adolescent child, however, may have a difficult time with an ISTJ parent – and vice versa.

ISTJs have a distrust for the fanciful, the ostentatious and the imaginative. They are 'no nonsense' types who are not attracted by anything remotely exotic. Instead they are always outstandingly practical and sensible. They live their lives by a series of 'shoulds'.

It is possible for ISTJs to acquire the social graces, ease with words and the necessary interpersonal skills to be so thoroughly outgoing that they are mistaken as Extraverts. All this will be in order to fulfil their sense of responsibility and duty. They can put on Extraverted clothing when the occasion demands without changing their essentially Introverted inner nature.

Nevertheless, for the ISTJ actions tend to speak louder than words. Their commitment to duty comes much less in saying and much more in doing. They care, and care deeply – and show it through their strong sense of responsibility which makes them very loyal to individuals and to institutions.

As long as they use their thinking to make judgements about inanimate objects and their sensing perception to understand human beings they will avoid making hasty judgements about, and riding over, other people. If they use their senses to see what is important to other folk, they may go to generous lengths to help.

ISFJ
Introverted Sensing with Feeling

The primary desire of ISFJ types is to be of service to other people. They are dependable, responsible people with a high sense of duty. They find their source of energy from within (Introversion) and perceive the world through what they can see, hear, touch, taste and smell. Their energy is then given in the service of others in an orderly, realistic and practical way.

When ISFJs see from their perception of the facts that something needs to be done, they willingly accept the responsibility. Factual accuracy is important to ISFJs and they prefer everything to be clearly stated. ISFJs take commitments and obligations very seriously, which can mean that others may take advantage of them.

They are quiet, reserved, steady, dependable and caring, and in their relationships – as with everything else – their strong sense of duty predominates. They gain satisfaction from attending to the needs of others. They tend to believe that work is good and that play has to be earned. They value and adhere to established routines and procedures and for the ISFJ there will always be some work which is yet to be completed.

Being a parent is a serious responsibility for the ISFJs. They tend to be hard-working, protective, devoted and patient, and will put the needs of their families before their own. They will expect their children to conform to society's norms and feel a personal duty to see that those rules are kept. Family events are very important: a chance to observe tradition and to express the importance of the family in action.

The private reactions of ISFJs can be intense, even unpredictable, but they will not be seen on their faces. Their inner reactions are seldom shown to others, but behind the outward calm appearance, they can look at things in an intensely individualistic and humorous way. But when they feel they are 'on duty' their behaviour is practical and sensible.

ISFJs are very good at all details that need to be done to complete a task. Persevering, hard-working and patient, they often choose careers which combine their careful observation with their care for people.

They can be suspicious of iNtuition and imagination and not value those kind of creative insights in others. In addition, if their Feeling judgement is not developed, they will be less effective in relating to the world, remaining so absorbed with their inner reactions that little is offered to those around them.

INFJ
Introverted iNtuition with Feeling

The dominant preference and driving force of INFJ types is their iNtuition, which is directed inwards and generates a flow of insights, meanings, patterns and ideas. The external world can interfere with this stream of inspiration because INFJs feel a duty to offer service to humanity in an orderly and regular manner.

INFJs are generally described as gentle, compassionate people, yet given to streaks of stubbornness. When they are committed to an objective or an ideal their stubbornness can emerge and these otherwise quiet, reserved characters can become rigid and demanding of themselves and others.

INFJs trust the insights which their iNtuition offers them into the true relationships and meaning of things. They tend to be independent and individualistic in their inner lives though this may not be readily apparent because of their desire for warm and harmonious relationships with others. They possess a quiet strength and their caring, concerned approach to life attracts other people to them. They can be effective, if unobtrusive, leaders, encouraging others to join with them and co-operate with their purposes. They tend to lead by gaining others' acceptance of their ideas.

They are fulfilled by work with people that satisfies their iNtuition and Feeling. Routine jobs do not satisfy, rather they will seek opportunities where their iNtuition can be combined with their feeling judgements.

INFJs tend to be there when they are needed, offering quiet stability and strength to people and situations. They can be hard to get to know, but they have a rich inner life. They like to please other people and find conflict disagreeable. They tend to be sensitive in the way they relate to others and work well in organizational structures which run smoothly and harmoniously. Their personal warmth, insight, originality and organizational abilities are all brought into play. They can be devastated by too much criticism and unpleasant working relationships can lead them to lose confidence.

The home provides INFJs with the stage on which to act out their idealism, their need to serve others and their longing for harmony. Parenthood means accepting the serious responsibility to help young minds to develop on their own. INFJ parents are fiercely devoted and will ensure that all their children are offered every opportunity for development, seeking to be stimulating and helpful in any way they can. It is important for the ethos of the home to be congenial, accepting and stimulating. INFJs are especially sensitive to family tension, having a tendency to personalize conflict and even blame themselves for some problems they did not cause.

In general, INFJs are good at helping others achieve their goals, always seeking to encourage the personal development of others.

The single-minded devotion to insights and ideas which is characteristic of INFJs can lead to problems if they fail to observe other factors that might conflict with the goal they are pursuing.

If their Feeling judgement is not developed, they will find it difficult to evaluate their inner vision and to hear feedback from other people. Instead of helping translate iNtuitive insights into effective actions, they may end up by seeking to structure, order and regulate everything in relation to their own ideas, so that little is accomplished.

INTJ
Introverted iNtuition with Thinking

People with INTJ type preferences tend to be the most independent of all types. They are the innovators of the world, seeking improvements in everything. Whatever is good can always be made better.

INTJs trust their iNtuitive insights into the meanings, patterns and inter-relationships of things. Problems and difficulties are challenges which exist to stimulate innovative responses. They value their iNtuitive insight and want to see their ideas worked out and come to fruition in practice.

INTJs find a natural place in organizations, often rising to positions of responsibility. They work long and hard in pursuit of their goals and they are interested in moving an organization forwards and onwards to a better future. They tend to see the 'big picture' – the forest as well as the trees (through their iNtuition) – and their Thinking judgement gives them the ability to complete all their undertakings. People expect any job with which INTJs are involved to be done well, and they are rarely disappointed.

INTJs possess determination and perseverance and they have a high regard for their own – and others' – competence. Their independence can lead others to view them as aloof. INTJs learn through exploration, discussion and the asking of questions, which is all part of their quest to understand the universe. They are the most theoretical of all types, but problems may arise if an INTJ's discussions and critical questions are regarded by others as hostile behaviour.

Other problems may arise from the INTJ's single-minded concentration on, and pursuit of, his/her objectives. INTJs may see their objectives and goals so clearly that they fail to take other views and possibilities into account. They may need to consciously seek the views of others.

INTJs love to see ideas and systems translated into realities. Decisions tend to come naturally to INTJs and they will be looking towards the future, rather than the past. INTJs will conform to rules if they are useful, but being the most innovative and theoretical of all types, they find no idea too far-fetched to be considered. They are natural brain-stormers, always seeking new concepts, ideas and ways ahead.

Their fellow workers can find them unemotional, cold and dispassionate and difficult to satisfy. If INTJs neglect their own feeling values, and ignore other people's, they may be surprised by the depth of the opposition they encounter. Their feeling needs to be used constructively, through their appreciation of other people and their contributions.

As parents, INTJs' desire for improvement can become a model for their children. The INTJ parent will encourage the self-sufficiency and independence of their children. They have high expectations of their performance yet encourage them to develop in directions of their own choosing.

INTJs use their Thinking preference to deal with the outside world and their dominant preference, iNtuition, may be seldom seen. If their Thinking judgement is undeveloped, they will be unable to shape their insights and inspirations into practical action.

ISTP
Introverted Thinking with Sensing

ISTP types may best be described as reserved and cautious. They prefer to focus inwards, and this tendency, combined with their logical, objective Thinking preference, means that they are more inclined to wait-and-see before declaring their hand. Their view of the world is concrete and specific, but combined with the open-ended way they relate through their Perception, this means that they can be more actively spontaneous than might be apparent at first sight.

They use their Thinking preference to discover the principles which underlie the information about the world they have perceived through their senses. They are logical, analytical, objective people who are unlikely to be convinced by anything other than reasoning which is based on solid, concrete facts. They like to organize facts and information rather than people or situations, and they can be cautious in their interpersonal relationships. Despite being somewhat quiet, even shy, they can converse at length on subjects which enable them to display their wealth of information.

ISTPs are especially skilled with their hands and receive satisfaction from the completion of specific, concrete tasks. They tend to like sport, the outdoors, indeed anything that provides information for their senses. When some*thing* needs attention, their powers of observation (if developed) enable them to have a firm grasp of the realities of the situation and to plunge into the task in hand. When the result is successful, ISTPs feel a great sense of achievement. They have a talent for seeing the important and unique facts of a situation. They are interested in how and why things work and they tend to have a mastery of tools of many kinds.

Because ISTPs alternate between an enthusiasm for things of immediate interest and quiet reserve about other things, their reactions and their relationships with people are difficult to predict. They can seem enigmatic to Extravert and Judging types.

Their nature is to be quietly observing, collecting data on all things at all times. But when an emergency occurs, they can move swiftly to the heart of the problem and deal with it. What seems like instinctive action is the result of long observation which enables ISTPs to be aware of all the details.

Routine work and administration is of little interest to ISTPs, whereas new, unexplored and unexpected elements are so energizing, they aren't thought of as work at all.

ISTP parents do not go in for long-term planning. They wait and see what each day brings and then do what is needed. They do not have a strong desire to impose themselves on their children and those living with an ISTP will enjoy a high level of personal freedom. ISTPs learn best by doing and need 'hands on' projects and practical experiments to keep them interested and involved.

Family events are a mixed blessing for ISTPs. They may eagerly anticipate special family events but the preparations often hold more interest than the social demands of the event itself. ISTPs may need to develop their Feeling values, and to express their appreciation of others. They have a tendency to put off decisions and if their Thinking judgement is less well developed, nothing of importance or value will be achieved.

47

ISFP
Introverted Feeling with Sensing

ISFP types are people with a great deal of personal warmth but they don't tend to show it until they know a person well. There is a love and sensitivity for others as well as a serenity and an appreciation of life. ISFPs can be more in touch with themselves and the world around them than any other type. When they care, they care deeply, but they are more likely to show it by actions rather than words.

ISFPs have no desire to lead and control others, but wish to see everyone and everything living harmoniously. They find it hard to understand why some people need to impose limits, order and structure upon others. They have little need to lead, or influence or change or control, or even understand the world. They simply take it all in. In their desire *not* to impress or impose themselves, ISFPs may be overlooked by others. They tend not to project a strong image, nor are they competitive by nature.

In everyday activities, they are tolerant, open-minded, flexible and adaptable, and usually enjoy the present moment. They are interested in the realities brought to them by their senses, and they have a special love of nature and a sympathy with animals. They are creative, artistic types who can excel in craftsmanship. The work of their hands speaks much more loudly than any words. Indeed, ISFPs are usually not interested in developing abilities and skills in speaking, writing or conversation. They take a personal approach to living, judging things by the personal values and ideals which govern their lives. These ideals may never be spoken or expressed in words. ISFPs are one of the kindest and most sympathetic of all types. They see the needs of the moment and try to meet them. The kind of work that suits them requires both devotion and adaptability. Their work has to contribute to things that matter to them and they tend to be perfectionists when they care deeply about something. A problem can arise if ISFPs feel a discrepancy between their inner ideals and their achievements, such that they burden themselves with a sense of personal inadequacy. They tend to take for granted the things they do well, and can underrate and understate themselves.

As parents, ISFPs welcome the opportunity to relate to their children rather than control them. It is possible that their children may not be given a basic sense of structure and order. The ISFP's low need for control or domination is intended to allow his/her children to grow more freely. Children learn that the ISFP parent is always near, in touch with the child's needs and very supportive of the child's development. Love is not so much spoken of, as displayed.

It is important for ISFPs to find practical actions through which to express their ideals; if they don't they can quickly lose confidence in themselves. In reality, they have a very great deal to offer, once they have found their right niche.

INFP
Introverted Feeling with iNtuition

INFP types take a personal approach to living, judging every-thing by their personal values and inner ideals. They discover their ideals through a subjective understanding of the world around them and their ideals are used to help others. They seek fulfilment through offering help and service to others and to society.

They stick to their ideals with passionate conviction, even though they may find these difficult to talk about. Their deepest feelings are rarely spoken. They tend to be easy-going, flexible and adaptable in everyday living, preferring to fit in harmoniously with those around them. But if their inner loyalties and values are threatened, the INFP can become very rigid, demanding and even aggressive. For those who don't understand this characteristic, the INFP can seem a source of mixed signals: easy-going and flexible one minute, rigid the next. Others can find them deeply complex people who are difficult to understand.

Apart from their commitment to their work, INFPs have little desire to impress, control or dominate others. Their main interest is in seeing the possibilities beyond what is present and they want their work to achieve something that matters deeply to them.

INFPs resist being labelled and are engaged in a never-ending search for self-knowledge and self-identity. 'Who am I?' is the all-important question. Their Introversion fosters inward reflection; their iNtuition prompts a sense of the endless possibilities inherent in the self; their Feeling guides them to reflect on how such potential can benefit themselves and others and their Perception keeps them open to a flow of new information. The

49

INFP's open-ended approach to life may produce far more questions than answers.

In general, home and family relationships are relaxed and flexible. An INFP parent is generally positive and affirming and quick to meet his/her children's needs. But they may feel far more warmth and love than they often show.

In general INFPs love to serve and please others, but they always feel they could have done better. Their easy-going exterior can mask a compulsive interior, and their need to be of service to others can prevent them from relaxing and enjoying themselves. Some INFPs can feel a sense of inadequacy and guilt because of the gap between the ideals they hold and their actual achievements: it is important for them to find ways of living out their insights and vision in actions.

INTP
Introverted Thinking with iNtuition

The inner reflectiveness of INTP types enables them to explore the imaginative possibilities provided by their iNtuition, which are then analysed objectively to discover the underlying principles. They rely on their Thinking to develop these principles and their logical, analytical approach maintains the focus on the ideas rather than on people.

INTPs prefer to organize ideas and knowledge rather than situations or people. They are intensely curious and are always seeking to make coherence out of an endlessly proliferating amount of data. The aim is to fit all the pieces into a complete picture which keeps expanding with the continuing discovery of new pieces. All thoughts, ideas and plans – however final they appear – are subject to last-minute changes when new information arises.

Any project presents itself as a mental challenge and the INTP thinks through every stage of the task in hand. This process is more exciting and challenging to the INTP than actually doing what needs to be done. INTPs can show the greatest precision in thought and language of all types. They are the 'architects' of systems, which are then left to others to build.

Socially, INTPs tend to have a small group of close friends with whom they enjoy discussing ideas and concepts. Although they are quiet and reserved, they can be talkative on a subject to which they have given a lot of thought. Their interest lies in seeing possibilities beyond what is present and known, by using their insight, ingenuity and intellectual ability.

One of the dangers for INTPs is that they gain too little knowledge and experience of the world around them. They may also find it hard to make their ideas understood by others. They may rely so much on logical analytical thinking that they overlook what other people care about. They dislike incoherence and value intelligence, which can make them impatient with those who are less able.

As parents, INTPs are patient with, and accepting of, the differences in children. They want, above all, to help young minds develop and grow. INTPs seek to open up new possibilities for their children, offering many alternatives.

Family events for INTPs are generally fun because they offer chances to explore what makes such events and people tick. While an INTP may fail to remember family anniversaries, such events are still important. At the very least, family occasions offer material for thought about the meaning of the family and its place in life.

Work that doesn't involve intellect and the opportunity for mastery soon becomes drudgery for INTPs. If a job doesn't offer new challenges, boredom and poor performance may result.

INTPs deal with the world, which exists primarily to be understood, through their iNtuition. Their dominant preference – Thinking – may remain relatively hidden except with close friends. Excelling at analysis, INTPs may have difficulty in expressing their appreciation of others.

ESTP
Extraverted Sensing with Thinking

ESTP types are oriented outwards to the external world of people and things, and their information is gathered through the reality of their five senses. The information so gathered is analysed objectively, whilst the ESTP remains open and flexible to any new alternatives. These four preferences combine to produce quick, practical, realistic responses to any situation.

51

ESTPs are adaptable realists, relying on what they see, hear and know at first hand. They seek realistic and satisfying solutions without imposing any 'shoulds' or 'oughts' of their own. Their adaptability means that they are good problem-solvers. They are resourceful people of action who live for the present moment. It is hard to get an ESTP to make plans and prepare thoroughly. They would rather be 'doing', and are not necessarily bound by previously established procedures or methods.

They will tend to learn from their personal experience rather than from study or reading, and ideas and theories aren't to be trusted until they have been tried out in experience.

Outgoing, realistic, flexible, fearless, ESTPs will try any challenge once. But once a job becomes routine, the ESTP may lose interest and move on to the next thing. They make good initiators of new projects, but may fail to persevere with the details and will need to have someone else on hand to take care of the follow up.

ESTPs are open-minded, tolerant people who can take things as they are. This means they can be good at easing tense situations and enabling competing and conflicting groups to come together. They enjoy life to the full. They are good companions and fun to be with. As parents, ESTPs have realistic expectations of their children and partners. It isn't necessary for their children to excel academically, but they must do something constructive and practical with their lives, which will make them happy.

ESTPs can be good innovators, negotiators and entrepreneurs. Always resourceful, their effectiveness will depend on how much personal fulfilment they receive from the current task. If their Thinking is well developed, they will be able to set standards for their behaviour and direction and purpose for their lives.

ESFP
Extraverted Sensing with Feeling

ESFPs are warm, open, realistic people who radiate optimism. They rely on their senses for their information about the external world and they accept and use the 'facts', whatever they are. They have no need to impose 'shoulds' and 'oughts' of their own on to situations or people, because they know that a solution will turn up once they have got all the facts together.

Their adaptability is used to solve problems and they can be good at getting others to adapt too. ESFPs are open-minded, tolerant, amusing and good company. Of all the 16 types, they are the ones who live for the moment. 'A bird in the hand is worth two in the bush', sums up their philosophy; when there's no 'bird', their energy is directed towards obtaining one.

Their focus on the immediate means they have a low tolerance for procedures, details and routines. Their combination of Extraversion, Sensing and Feeling leads ESFPs to try and make each moment a satisfying personal experience. They are very accepting of others in their desire for happy relationships, but may ignore or deny anything that threatens the harmony they seek. Conflict tends to be avoided rather than engaged with creatively. The ESFP's joy of living is contagious and he/she seeks the company of others whenever possible. The home of an ESFP is likely to be filled with people who are having a good time. ESFPs are very generous, giving help and assistance to others without expecting any return.

ESFPs prefer active jobs and they love working with people. Decisions are made with people in mind and rely heavily on personal experience. In their work ESFPs make more starts than finishes and they will need someone else to follow through with the details. They are less interested in scholastic pursuits than some other types yet knowledge is important for its immediate usefulness.

Their sheer adaptability means that ESFPs have an uncanny skill for making life into a three-ringed circus, juggling many activities and people and enjoying the hustle and bustle and the limelight. As parents they can pack half a dozen activities for their children into a single evening. Exciting for all those involved, it can leave others and especially their children (if of different types) exhausted by the process. Children who find life with ESFP parents tiring, will, nevertheless, enjoy their warm, supportive, easy-going ways. The problem is that there may not be enough direction or discipline around the home, or sufficient planning for the future.

How effective they are depends (like ESTPs) on how much Judgement they have. If their Feeling is well developed, their values will provide standards, direction and purpose for their lives. But if their Judgement is less well developed there is a danger that ESFPs will opt for their love of a good time.

ENFP
Extraverted iNtuition with Feeling

People with ENFP preferences are enthusiastic, ingenious, imaginative and dynamic, with highly developed interpersonal skills. They have the ability to deal with a variety of situations, people and events, often at the same time.

ENFPs are good innovators, always aware of new possibilities and new ways of doing things. Their imaginative perception gives them energy for starting lots of new projects. Difficulties serve to act as stimulations for new problem-solving. ENFPs can become so absorbed in their latest project or challenge that they have no time for anything else. Their enthusiasm is contagious and their world is full of possible schemes. Indeed, they can see so many possible projects they may have difficulty choosing between them. For ENFPs routine is bad news. They can find it hard to concentrate on the small details and they may get bored with their own projects quickly so that as soon as the main problem has been dealt with and the initial challenge responded to, the ENFP is on to the next new thing. They may need to learn to see things through to completion or provide the organization and other people to finish what they have started.

The ENFP's Feeling preference shows itself in a care of people. They are skilled in relating with others, showing acute perception and insight. They aim to understand rather than judge others and always seek to be positive about others' potential. They have a high need to be affirming of others *and* to receive affirmation from others in return.

ENFPs have an infectious enthusiasm for living. Being a parent is fun and their home is likely to be a playground for creative adventure. Family events for ENFPs quickly turn into parties and their home is a gathering place for neighbours and friends. It has been said that the Irish wake was probably designed by an ENFP who preferred to celebrate a life rather than mourn a death.

For the ENFP work too must become play, or it is probably not worth doing. ENFPs are good improvisers and they can and do go to great lengths to please others. Because they are drawn to the exciting challenges of new possibilities their Feeling judgement will need to be developed. If it isn't, there is a danger that ENFPs will be drawn to many different projects, fail to complete anything and allow their energies, inspirations and insights to be diminished by not completing their tasks.

ENTP
Extraverted iNtuition with Thinking

ENTP types are ingenious, inventive people who are always discovering new possibilities and are aware of new ways of doing things. Their inventiveness is due to their iNtuition which gives them their imaginative ideas, combined with their objective Thinking which is directed outwardly to the external world. Everything is converted into possibilities, ideas, plans and schemes and their initiative and imagination leads ENTPs to start many new projects. Like most EPs they are more excited about trying out a new idea and plan than they are of continuing with an existing scheme.

ENTPs find problems stimulating and their ingenuity loves to tackle complex situations. Their ability to see the larger picture enables them to think up many alternatives for any system – whether family, an organization, a stamp collection, or a holiday. ENTPs are aware that any procedure or system, no matter how good, can always be made better. Their enthusiasm leads them into a variety of activities and they enjoy being competent in all of them.

ENTPs enjoy and are stimulated by doing the unexpected or the unusual. Like most NTs they learn by challenging discussion and they are capable of arguing both sides of a subject for the stimulation it gives them.

They are perceptive about the attitudes and views of others, always seeking to understand others rather than to judge them. In relationships with ENTPs we can expect to be challenged, usually by what is new or exciting or different. They will always be stimulating companions.

Their energy comes from a variety of new projects and interests. They may show interest in so many different things that they have difficulty focusing. But their Thinking can provide the necessary critical analysis for their iNtuitions and inspiration so that the right projects can be selected.

The ENTP sees family life as an opportunity for the personal growth and development of every member. The home of an ENTP may be full of the latest books, videos, games, gadgets.

55

Children will be introduced to everything possible, so that they can be challenged and their minds stretched and enriched. Many ENTP parents will generate far more ideas, possibilities and plans in one afternoon than their children will ever be able to manage. The emphasis is on challenge, new ideas, possibilities and opportunities, and their encouragement of independent thinking characterizes the ENTP's style of life.

Like everything else, family gatherings and evenings with friends are chances to share ideas. The easy-going nature and good humour of ENTPs make them attractive companions and they are likely to have a wide circle of friends.

One of the difficulties for ENTPs is that they dislike humdrum routine and can find it hard to apply themselves to the necessary detail. They can get bored and restless with their own projects, once the major challenge has been solved, and they may well need others to see things through to completion. They are happiest in jobs which allow them to exercise their ingenuity as they tackle one project after another. Because they are always drawn to the excitement of new challenges and possibilities, it is important that they develop their Judgement: otherwise they may undertake less than important projects, fail to finish them and waste their ingenuity and imagination on unfinished tasks.

ESTJ
Extraverted Thinking with Sensing

ESTJ types perceive the world 'as it is' through their Sensing and deal with those perceptions objectively through their Thinking. They are born organizers and seek to order the world around them with structures and schedules. They use their Thinking to organize and manage as much of the world as they can. They tend to be logical, analytical and, above all, organized.

ESTJs are outstanding at organizing orderly procedures, rules and regulations, and they can be impatient with those who don't carry out their tasks and keep to the rules.

ESTJs are seen by others as practical, dependable and able to get things done. They tend to end up in the top positions of any organization. Their desire for control leads them always to say 'Yes' when asked to assume positions of responsibility.

They tend to be realistic and matter of fact about things and are more curious about new devices and gadgets and processes than about new principles and theories. They use past experience to help them solve problems and getting things done is their strong suit.

ESTJs are generally dutiful and loyal to their organizations, communities and families. They see where their duty lies and are dependable and consistent in fulfilling it.

They may not always respond to views which differ from their own and they may jump to conclusions too quickly. ESTJs may need to make a special effort to remain open to the ideas and views of others. They find it hard to understand or sympathize with those who seek radical change.

ESTJs follow established routines well at home and at work, tending to have a place for everything and wanting everything in its place. They are usually neat, tidy and orderly at work and at play.

ESTJ parents tend to have sharply defined roles for themselves and their children, and when family members respond to ESTJ expectations, things go smoothly for all concerned. Home, family, parenting are among the key commitments of ESTJs' life. Family life is one more thing to manage. Hard work, timed schedules and merit-based rewards are hallmarks of ESTJ life. Fun, relaxation and free time are scheduled and dished out – both to self and others. Good work brings its own rewards.

Family events are important to ESTJs and must be honoured with loyal obedience. ESTJs look forward to birthdays, anniversaries, family reunions. Although they might protest about attending such events, it would never occur to them not to be present.

Two slogans describe the attitude of ESTJs: 'If it isn't broken, don't fix it', and, 'Anything worth doing is worth doing well'.

Because of their decisive, loyal approach to people and situations, ESTJs may need to take more account of the views of others. If they can learn to listen, to take Feeling values into account and to express their appreciation of other people, they will be rewarded in both their working and family lives.

ESFJ
Extraverted Feeling with Sensing

ESFJ types bring harmony and goodwill to any situation in which they find themselves. Their concern is for the well-being of the people around them and they are especially sensitive to individual needs. They are friendly and sympathetic, gracious and effective in dealing with others.

ESFJs are the great nurturers of established institutions – home, school, church, civic groups and societies – and are immensely loyal to respected persons or causes, sometimes to the point of idealizing those people and organizations they admire. Traditions are carefully observed and maintained by ESFJs.

ESFJs are hurt by indifference and need to be appreciated for themselves and for the services they offer others. ESFJs have a set of values which contain many 'shoulds' and 'oughts', 'should nots' and 'ought nots', and they may express these freely.

They can find it difficult to face up to difficulties when there are problems with people or things they care about. They may overlook disagreeable facts in a situation and, if they do, the problem will be swept under the carpet rather than a solution sought.

ESFJs are mainly interested in the realities perceived by their five senses. They are practical, realistic, down-to-earth people. They are at their best in jobs that involve people, where co-operation is achieved through goodwill. They are less likely to be happy in work which demands abstract concepts and theoretical analysis.

Compassion, awareness, caring, warmth, harmonious relationships are everything. ESFJs are conscientious home-makers and providers. They enjoy socializing and entertaining – albeit in a scheduled, orderly and appropriate manner – and parties are great, when sufficiently planned.

Appropriateness is another key word for ESFJs and their children. The child of an ESFJ parent probably feels loved and generally satisfied, although somewhat restricted by the 'shoulds' and 'oughts' of their parents, and the need to put work before play.

ESFJs tend to be loyal in their family relationships, often sacrificing their own needs for the sake of the other family members. They usually respect and revere their parents and are able to express the right feelings in any given situation. They can be soft-hearted and sentimental and often observe birthdays and anniversaries with a flourish.

ENFJ
Extraverted Feeling with iNtuition

The focus and attention of ENFJ types is directed towards other people and they are skilled in understanding the needs and motivation of others. Additionally, their gift for imagination and intuition is expressed in an orderly organised way which allows them to turn their ideas into reality.

ENFJs are born co-operators. They communicate sympathy, caring and concern and a willingness to become involved. They place a high value on harmonious relationships and it is not surprising that people turn to ENFJs for encouragement, nurture and support. At times these demands can threaten to overwhelm ENFJs who find it almost impossible to say 'No', even when the demands are unreasonable. ENFJs are tolerant of other people, seldom critical and always trustworthy.

ENFJs are very accomplished at working with individuals and groups and can quickly find themselves in leadership positions. Yet ENFJs can become depressed and hurt if their ideas are met with indifference or criticism. They take conflict and rejection personally and disagreements can escalate out of all proportion. If the iNtuition of an ENFJ is well developed s/he would do well to follow his/her hunches. Decisions made purely on the basis of logic may not be so sound and checking these out with someone who has a clear Thinking preference might be advisable. ENFJs are good at 'reading' people and situations. Seldom is an ENFJ wrong about the motivations or intent of another person whether it's hidden or not.

ENFJs are socially adept, even-tempered and tireless in their efforts to bring about peace and well-being. ENFJs tend to have as an ideal the perfect relationship and their longing for this in marriage as in other spheres of life can result in a sense of vague dissatisfaction with the way things are.

ENFJs are always interested in seeing the possibilities beyond the present. INtuition heightens their curiosity for new ideas and insights. They are at their best in jobs which deal with people and situations that demand co-operative working. Impersonal tasks and work demanding factual accuracy are much less congenial unless they can find some personal meaning in the work.

ENFJs like their work and their social engagements settled and organized. They are usually charming and popular wherever they are, not least because of their fluency in speech.

For an ENFJ being a parent is a responsibility and a pleasure. Young lives are waiting to be directed and channelled by the ENFJ's value system. Children will know where an ENFJ parent stands on most things and how they are expected to behave. ENFJs have many 'shoulds' and 'oughts'. When behaviour is good, parental affirmation overflows. But when it is bad, the ENFJ parent will feel a failure, which in turn can give the child a sense of guilt about failing to please the parent.

When harmony is present, life in an ENFJ household can be lively and fun. But there must be order before relaxation, and fun is always balanced by a good measure of work.

Any opportunity to be with others, to serve others, to entertain others will be taken by ENFJs. But like ESFJs they find it hard to admit the truth about difficulties and problems with people or situations. Failure to face up to disagreeable facts will mean that problems are ignored rather than solutions sought.

ENTJ
Extraverted Thinking with iNtuition

The energy of ENTJ types is directed outwardly to a world full of meanings (iNtuition) which are analysed objectively into systems in a timely and orderly fashion (Judging). They use their Thinking to order and manage as much of the world as they can, enjoying executive, active and long-range planning. They are logical, analytical, objectively critical and only likely to be convinced by reasoning. They concentrate on ideas, rather than the people behind the ideas.

ENTJs tend to give structure and organization wherever they are and harness ideas and people to long-range goals. They resemble ESTJ types in their willingness to establish plans for a task or organization but ENTJs search more for policy and goals than for regulations and procedures. ENTJs are happy with established procedures but they can abandon any procedure when it doesn't serve the intended goal. They are impatient with inefficiency and incompetence and can be tough when situations call for it. For the ENTJ there always must be a reason for doing anything and people's feelings aren't normally sufficient. Details and interpersonal skills are not the ENTJ's strong points. They are mainly interested in seeing the possibilities beyond the present. Intuitions heighten their intellectual interest.

In charge of an organization, ENTJs are able to offer long-term vision and to communicate that vision to others. They are gifted with language, and clarity of thought and speech make them excellent communicators. They are natural organizers and find themselves in command through their ability to plan and keep both long-and short-term objectives clearly in mind. They enjoy being executives and usually rise to positions of responsibility – although they may need someone around with enough common sense to bring up overlooked facts and take care of important details.

As at work, so at home: when an ENTJ is present there will be little doubt as to who is in charge. Family members will know their responsibilities within the system. Family events are fun, and provide another chance to plan, organize and lead.

Like other decisive types ENTJs can run the risk of deciding things too quickly and they may need to stop and listen to the views of others. They may need to work at taking feeling values into account – especially those of other people – and learn to express their appreciation of others.

4 | The Beginning, Not The End

Once our type has been discovered, it should not be thought that this is the 'end of the road'. There is a great deal that can still be explored to gain further understanding, to work on our less-preferred functions, and to explore how our type relates to other types in a wide range of situations. To begin that process, this chapter is devoted to giving advice: it takes the form of a series of suggestions written for each of the eight possible letters denoting the type formulae.

Suggestions to Extraverts

First of all, appreciate yourself as a person who can get along with others, who can get things done and who likes action and vitality. *Appreciate yourself* is the most important advice that can be given to anyone. Like all other Extraverts, you also need affirmation from others; there is nothing wrong with this, so don't be afraid to ask for it if it is not forthcoming!

When dealing with Introvert types try to be careful to respect their needs and not to 'assault' them with your out-goingness. Try not to invade their privacy: accept the fact that they are different from you and that they re-charge their batteries in different ways. Don't expect Introverts to come up with information without you asking for it; you need to draw them out, giving them time to consider your questions – and their replies.

As Extraverts tend to think aloud, recognize that your first words on a subject may not be your final ones; they are what you see them as, *first* words. Introverts, though, operate in a different way and they may assume that you have given as much thought to your words as they themselves have to theirs, which will probably not be the case.

Extraverts need to remember to listen; they are prone to be inveterate talkers. They are also likely to come over to Introverts as overwhelming, intrusive and demanding; try to hold back a bit and don't feel that you have to fill every space, and remember, silence can be golden!

Recognize that as an Extravert you often do your best work when thinking aloud, so use this to your advantage. Try to work alongside people with whom you can check out your ideas – but remember, you may need to learn to listen to them as well, for perhaps they need to check their ideas out with you too.

Remember to work on your least-preferred function, give it a chance to develop, and recognize what your introverted auxiliary has to offer. Allow yourself time to be quiet and reflect, there is also a place for introversion in Extraverts. Be grateful for all the good things that Extraverts can enjoy and ensure that you make the most of them.

Suggestions to Introverts

Appreciate yourself as a person with real depth, who is interesting to get to know. As you keep your best to yourself, you must work on extraverting your auxiliary so that the outside world has something to observe and latch on to.

It probably comes as a relief to discover that it is quite natural for you to have difficulties in relating quickly and easily to the outer world of people and events, of action and interaction. There is nothing *wrong* with you! Extraverts, remember, have *need* for social interaction and so they 'arrange' things so that their style of behaviour appears to be the norm.

As an Introvert there is always a danger that you think that you have said things and communicated rather more than you actually have. You may have spent a long time thinking about something and working things out in your head, but unless you actually tell someone, no one will know. It may seem a strange thing to say, but Introverts should endeavour to smile more. They often fail to show their feelings or affection, and whilst at times this can be a considerable strength, life is seldom as serious as many Introverts tend to suggest by their body language.

In relating to Extraverts you may have to explain your need for privacy and time to think. They will not immediately realize this, as Extraverts tend to do their thinking whilst they are talking rather than sorting things out in their mind first. So you may need to tell them that you are thinking as they might easily conclude that they have said something wrong if you are quiet and then they try to fill the gap with more words. Another thing about

Extraverts: they tend to need affirming, and it would be good if you could learn to express appreciation to them on a regular basis.

This may be quite difficult: if you could find an Extravert with whom you could talk things through it could be of considerable help to both of you. It would enable you to understand the Extravert environment better, and would give you practice in expressing things in ways which they can understand. It may seem unfair, but the onus is on you if you want people to understand something that is important to you. If you live with an Extravert make sure that you still have some capacity for extraversion left in you when you get home from work. Don't disappear into your own private world the moment you walk through the door!

Above all, be grateful for the strengths and gifts which come with being an Introvert. You are able to handle solitude, you can have remarkable depth, and you have a great deal to offer to other people.

Suggestions to iNtuitives

INtuitives should appreciate themselves for their creativity, for their ability to see possibilities in so many things and in so many situations, and for their insight. Being an iNtuitive can be great fun and has enormous potential. Perhaps the most telling advice that can ever be given to an iNtuitive is 'When all else fails, read the instructions'!

When dealing with Sensers, remember that they take facts and details more seriously than you do, and that these are more important to them than all the possibilities and ideas that you may present. When you have a good idea for solving some problem, make sure that you have spelled out the problem to a Senser before you provide him or her with a solution.

It is important that iNtuitives finish their sentences – and allow others to finish theirs without finishing them for them. Also, take care to define your terms: iNtuitives are marvellous at broad sweeps, but can sometimes struggle when it comes to detail. Remember that Sensers are not impressed by the big sweep, nor are they impressed by you having a hundred different ideas; try to whittle them down to just one or two!

If you are having to present a case to a Senser, you might try writing it down first, to see if it flows sequentially (Sensers have problems with an argument which is presented like a bouncing ball, touching the earth occasionally and then rising to new heights in different places!).

INtuitive types need to make sure that they take care of their body as they can too easily suffer from burn-out in pursuit of some new project. They also need to take time to enjoy the present, and not be so engrossed with the future that the present passes them by. If you can't find something, look again, and again – it will almost certainly be in a place that you have already searched through; better still, ask a Senser to look for you!

INtuitives are great hoarders, so try to throw something away every day. Force yourself to notice details, remember that your least preferred function is your Sensing, so try to enjoy what you can see or hear, feel or touch. Practise working on some fine details – figure-work, photography, keeping a diary, or attend to your files which are probably in a state of considerable disarray!

Be thankful for the wonderful world of possibilities that opens before you. The world needs people with ideas and imagination, and if you can marshall them in some sort of order so that others can cope with them, you will find it immensely rewarding.

Suggestions to Sensers

Appreciate yourself for your powers of observation, practical skills and sense of responsibility. You have the ability to 'knuckle down' to a job in hand, and to deal with all the minutiae of a process which many people find irksome or beyond them.

When dealing with iNtuitive types, let them feel that there are some interesting possibilities ahead before requiring them to get down to basic work. When you are communicating with an iNtuitive, stress your main point and don't overburden him/her with details – s/he is seldom interested in 'the fine print' and will just want to know the overall picture.

Sensers can easily get stuck in a rut, so try to do something new each day – even if it's just walking on the other side of the road or buying a different newspaper. Next time you think that there are massive problems ahead, try to enlist the help of an iNtuitive to help talk them through with you; you will be amazed at how differently s/he surveys the scene. When you are about to turn down an idea, give it one more chance and ask yourself 'What is needed to make it work?'.

Sensers can easily be locked into a very down-to-earth view of things, so allow your imagination to run riot sometimes. Look at a book like Bill Zimmerman's *Make Beliefs*[1] which invites you to consider such questions as 'Make believe that you could pluck the stars from the night sky to wear in your hair . . . what would you put in their place?' and 'Make believe that your meal consisted only of flowers . . . what would be for dinner?'

A piece of advice which I came across recently said 'If you are married to an iNtuitive type who thinks that your body is better than you think it is, accept it. He or she really does see you that way'. Sensers like treats which appeal to their sense of taste, or sound or sight, so make sure that you go out for a meal occasionally or see a good film, and enjoy your CD player.

Sensers tend to have a keen eye and can be fascinated by details. Be thankful for that, for there is a great deal which other types simply never notice, and their lives are impoverished as a result. Enjoy the special gifts that you have.

Suggestions to Feelers

Appreciate yourself for being a friendly, caring person with a strong sense of personal values and a great desire for harmony and friendship. In a world that tends to place economics and money above people you have an important contribution to make: your special gift of insight into how people feel or might be affected is greatly needed and appreciated.

You need to continue to affirm people, but make sure that your affirmation is *appropriate*. There is an enormous difference between a friendly look coupled with a word in season and constant gushing. You will need to come to terms with the fact that harmony is not always possible in all situations, that sometimes conflict is inevitable and it can be creative and (good news to you) therapeutic. You will also need to come to terms with the fact that not everyone will like you all the time. Whatever you do, it will not please everyone! This is a hard lesson for Feelers to come to terms with, and it does not help to start blaming yourself and trying to convince yourself that if you had done something else then the situation would not have arisen, and then perhaps all would have been well, and you would have been liked!

You need to realize that when Thinkers make impersonal comments, they are *not criticizing you as a person*. A critical comment about your work, your point of view or your hat does *not* mean that you are no longer accepted in your totality as a person, neither does it mean that you are not loved or regarded, and it does not mean that some other part of your work, some other views you have expressed or that your other hats are also being criticized.

Try to stand outside situations rather more often. Identification with others can be a great gift but it can also be a trial – not only to others, but also to yourself; admit it! Just because you are a Feeler, it does not mean that you cannot be logical and objective; and remember, that if you are, then Thinkers will appreciate you even more!

You may need to state your wishes rather more clearly. Feelers have a great capacity for burying their own desires, and they are prone to seek the role of sacrificial lamb. They can also be extremely manipulative. Think about taking assertiveness training. When you do state your own wishes, or opinions, try to keep them brief; Feelers have a tendency to repeat themselves as they are so concerned to make sure that they have been understood.

Don't assume that everyone else is as aware of feelings as you are, but do remember that other people may have different value systems which are just as important to them as yours are to you. Be thankful for your gifts of caring and sensitivity, there will always be a need for people who can befriend, or who want to understand others; peacemakers are in short supply in many situations.

Suggestions to Thinkers

Appreciate yourself for your logical mind, your ability to think things through to a conclusion, and for your critical faculties, your concern for fairness and justice and your dislike of fuzziness and emotionalism. Thinkers are not always the most popular people to have around, but they are essential if we are to avoid losing our way.

When dealing with Feeling types, remember that they like harmony, and would like to agree with you, so begin your discussions with points of agreement. This means that there is some sort of relationship established and when points of disagreement occur there is more of a chance that they can be discussed rather than fought over. Feelers are primarily interested in people and how things affect them, so endeavour to start with a concern for people, and you will discover that you are listened to more sympathetically. Remember also that Feelers may be less interested in reaching a logical conclusion and more interested in being listened to sympathetically and non-judgementally. Apply your mind to how you relate to Feelers! This will probably have the effect that you formulate your opinions, or solutions to problems, in ways that are agreeable to the people concerned.

Don't forget to come to terms with the vast amount of illogicality around you. Getting annoyed by it won't help, and will merely add to the emotional or irrational behaviour of others. Try to appreciate people a little more, and find ways of praising them and expressing your appreciation of their work, ideas, contribution . . . whatever – just take the trouble to affirm people. And try to smile more often, it can work wonders!

As a Thinking type, you are prone to be very critical; try to cut back on unnecessary criticisms and try to temper truth with mercy. Don't call people stupid because of the stupid things they do, try to discover *why* they did things in that way, and sort out the problem at that level. In the film *A Fish Called Wanda* nothing infuriates one of the characters more than being called stupid, and there is a delightful scene in which John Cleese is held upside down by his feet out of a window, high above the street, until he apologizes for calling this person stupid, even though he had done some rather stupid things. Remember, what you say may not be what people actually hear!

Try to concentrate a little more on the process; very often Thinkers are more interested in the conclusion, but others around them may have invested quite a lot in the process which is necessary to reach that conclusion. Sensitivity training might help you a great deal, both in your work situation and in your personal life.

Thinking types should use their Thinking function on their car and their Feeling function on their family – not the other way round! At its best, Thinking is logical and clear, at its worst it is carping criticism. Remember that your least preferred function is your Feeling so find ways of enabling yourself to express feelings – it is not a sign of weakness nor need it be illogical.

In a complex society such as ours, it is easy to lose sight of what is really important, and it is all too easy to forget what we are actually trying to do. The contribution that Thinkers can make is of enormous value and importance, but they are often their own worst enemies. Enjoy the gifts that you bring, but recognize that other people have different gifts and that they are not all Thinkers.

Suggestions to Judgers

Appreciate yourself for your organizational and planning skills, your dependability and loyalty and your commitment to finishing a job once you have begun it. These are all gifts upon which the whole of our social fabric depends.

Judgers need to have things ordered and under control; this can be liberating to others, or it can be tyrannical! Be aware of what you are doing to others, and in particular to the fact that you can drive Perceivers crazy. When making decisions try to involve others, and make sure that you have not acted too quickly. Have you explored other possibilities? Are there other conclusions which could be reached? Does it have to be settled right NOW? Try not to jump to conclusions; Judgers can sometimes give the impression that consultation is a farce – this is particularly apparent in family situations, when dealing with children, and in some team situations at work.

Recognize that your need for control and order may spring from your own inner insecurities, it may not be so much a strength as a weakness. Try to relax more, and take time off. If you are too busy, then plan for time off and put it in your diary. Try to remember that the world, society and Grubchester Cricket Club will not fall apart if you don't have everything sorted out. Few things depend solely upon one person, and it is a fact of life and death, that no one is indispensable.

When one of your plans falls through, it is all right to be upset. Looking at it this way gives you the opportunity to start on a new plan. When working with others recognize that they may have their own time scale and plans, so try to allow them to contribute, and allow yourself the luxury of changing your mind.

Reflect on some of the good things which have happened in your life which took you by surprise. Think of people you love but who are 'impossible' in terms of meeting deadlines or organizing things, and recognize that there is more to life than orderliness and decisions. Try asking the Perceivers in your family or at work to contribute to the decisions that you have to make, although recognize that this won't come easily to you but that it could be worth the effort.

Very often Judgers can give the impression that they have no doubts, and that they are certain in all their views; try sometimes to share your doubts or your hesitations, you will take people pleasantly by surprise.

You have real gifts in being able to make decisions and in being the sort of person people can rely upon. It doesn't always mean that you will be in a leadership position, but very often you will, and if your leadership is allied to imagination and sensitivity then you have a very great deal to offer.

Suggestions to Perceivers

Appreciate yourself for your flexibility and adaptability, for your spontaneous approach to life and your capacity to cope with the unexpected. In times of rapid social change such as ours, these are very considerable gifts.

Perceivers must recognize that they tend to drive Judgers round the bend! They cannot cope with your approach to deadlines, your tendency to procrastinate, your apparently cavalier attitude towards serious things and your scepticism of established order and hierarchical structures – in fact, with all those things which make it so interesting to be a Perceiver. Instead of shrugging your shoulders and explaining that that is their problem, see if you can meet them at least a little way down the path. Plan extra time so that you can really be *on time* with some things; give yourself early deadlines and endeavour to meet them (even if you are late, you might make the *actual* deadline). Learn some time-management techniques, and try to establish some routine in your life. Try to make some decisions quickly, though you will probably need to practise this!

Try to throw something away every day: Perceivers are great hoarders, and if they are also iNtuitives, their rooms, office, home or car might well contain enough material for half a dozen other people! Try to reduce the vast number of options that you have; see if it is possible to evaluate them and draw up a list of priorities. Recognize that the most immediate is not necessarily the most important. Perhaps you need to be more assertive, and could benefit from assertiveness training. Try to say 'No' rather more often and make fewer promises.

Perceivers are easily deflected from the task in hand; recognize this and set yourself some simple, manageable objectives. For instance, as a Perceiver, I have had to discipline myself not to go and make a cup of coffee each time I reached the end of writing one of these sections.

Perceivers know that it takes considerable skill to manage a complex life without a plan – something that Judgers will never understand. Enjoy the interesting life that being a Perceiver brings with it, enjoy the variety of interests and diversions that come your way, and recognize that, with just a little bit of discipline and routine the Perceiver's lot is, indeed, a very happy one.

5 | Needing Each Other

If it is accepted that no one type has all the gifts, and yet every type has some gifts, then it is obvious that we need each other. We all have something valuable to contribute, and we are all in need of the contributions that others can make. This is true in our personal relationships, it is true in our places of work and it is true in our social and leisure groups. If some of the greatest composers who ever lived found that they needed the bent piece of metal we call a triangle to add to the fullness of their symphonies, then there can be no doubting that each of us has something to offer and to add to the rich mixture of life.

One of the values of the Myers Briggs Type Indicator (MBTI) is that it can begin to identify just what it is that one person has to offer to another. Instead of being faced with the despairing question 'What have I got that is of any use?', and not quite knowing how to respond, a knowledge of personality type can help us to pinpoint and make explicit precisely what it is that people can offer. It can also help us have confidence when we are faced by people who seem to overwhelm us by their apparent omnicompetence, for no one is 'sufficient unto themself'.

Extraverts need Introverts

- To keep them focused and not deflected by external stimuli
- To explore inner depths
- To provide depth and concentration on shared tasks
- To help them value and deal with solitude
- To help them become aware of what's going on inside themselves
- To help them listen to others
- To help them with long slow jobs

Introverts need Extraverts

- To help them make their views known in discussions
- To help them know and be known
- To keep conversations flowing
- To ensure that strangers are welcomed
- To break the ice in social situations

Although we can all operate in an extraverted and in an introverted mode, we prefer one rather than the other, and as time passes, we rely upon others to meet and deal with those areas that we find difficult.

iNtuitives need Sensers

- To bring relevant facts to their attention
- To read the instructions, or the fine print in a contract
- To have patience and perseverance
- To apply a dose of realism to problems, and dreams
- To value what is on offer in the here and now
- To keep abreast of the essential details
- To keep records and to know where things are
- To notice what needs doing NOW
- To remind them that life is for living and enjoying now

Sensers need iNtuitives

- To develop a vision of the future and of what might be
- To tackle difficulties with ingenuity and relish
- To interpret and anticipate change
- To have enthusiasm
- To suggest new possibilities when faced by a problem
- To be on the look-out for new essentials
- To live with alternatives
- To remind them that the joys of the future are worth anticipating and working for

Each one of us is part Senser and part iNtuitive, but we prefer one to the other. If one of these is our dominant function, then the other will be our least-preferred and we may have gone to considerable lengths to avoid facing up to what it has to say to us.

Feelers need Thinkers

- To help them analyse facts and situations
- To help with organizational matters
- To do the 'unpleasant jobs' where people are concerned
- To stand firm when opposition grows
- To find flaws
- To restructure or reform
- To hold to a policy when it is strongly criticised

Thinkers need Feelers

- To keep the 'human factor' in view
- To conciliate and to persuade
- To advise how people will feel about things
- To build up enthusiasm
- To appreciate them as Thinkers

Once again, because we are all part Feeler and part Thinker, we will recognize these lists, and will probably be aware of those parts which we have chosen to ignore, or at least which we prefer not to capitalize on. It is, therefore, a comfort to know that the very things that we prefer not to deal with, others actually prefer to deal with, and that in those areas in which we are stronger, others look to us for help and support. It has been said that whilst we all have feelings, Feelers prefer to experience them whilst Thinkers prefer to understand them.

Perceivers need Judgers

- To help them come to a decision
- To provide some structure and routine
- To remind them of loyalty to their roots
- To give them a sense of time, and its passing
- To help them prepare for deadlines
- To see the benefits that can come from an ordered lifestyle
- To remind them that there are some ultimate authorities
- To ensure that necessary jobs get done

Judgers need Perceivers

- To help them not be too hasty
- To appreciate the variety of options that exists
- To see that a setback need not be a disaster
- To save them from the tyranny of routine
- To help them see rules as servants rather than masters
- To keep authorities and hierarchies in perspective
- To appreciate how much time there actually is
- To have fun and respond to the needs of the moment

We have both Judging and Perceiving in our make-up, but we prefer one to the other. Having decided on that preference, probably quite unconsciously, we will have developed that particular attitude and quite probably left the other dormant. We therefore need the help and support of others who have expressed a different preference.

The clearest vision of the future will usually come from an iNtuitive, whereas the most practical realism will come from a Senser. Thinkers tend to provide us with the most penetrating analysis whereas Feelers are usually the most skilful in handling people. Almost any enterprise that you can think of requires an assortment of skills, and it is highly probable that it will need a variety of personality types to provide them. When people approach a common task from a different starting point, there is likely to be a rich mixture of insight which can be highly creative. There are also likely to be problems of communication and understanding unless people are sensitive to the differing gifts that others may bring and also to those areas where they are likely to be in need of some sort of support. *There is a mutuality of gifts, a mutual usefulness of opposing types.*

Combining letters

We come now to an area of potential confusion. Anyone attending a Myers Briggs Workshop or reading the available literature will almost certainly have come across various combinations of letters being grouped together. Thus, instead of there being sixteen different responses to situations, one for each type, we find that often there are just four, reached by combining some of the groups. Which groups are combined, and why, is the result of a great deal of speculation and theoretical debate.

The most widely used of these groupings is that put forward by the Americans David Keirsey and Marilyn Bates and popularized in their book *Please Understand Me*[1]. Keirsey and Bates were brought up in a different psychological school from many of the people who were developing the Myers Briggs Indicator (they were Behaviourists rather than Jungian) and so they added their own 'touch' to it whilst at the same time being fully committed to using it in their clinical work. The internal differences should not bother us here, and we will use their concept of *'temperament'* as a helpful tool as we continue to look at how the MBTI can be used to enlarge our understanding of ourselves and others. Keirsey and Bates separated out the iNtuitive – Thinking (NT), iNtuitive – Feeling (NF), Sensing – Judging (SJ), and Sensing – Perceiving (SP) types.

Another method is to divide up the Type Table (see p. 33) into its four quadrants, this then gives us a different set of letters – IN (Introvert – iNtuitive), EN (Extravert – iNtuitive), IS (Introvert – Sensing) and ES (Extravert – Sensing). What is emerging is the realization that once we have the sixteen Types we can combine some of those which share common characteristics and find that they give us insights into different sorts of personality behaviour, and that we can often recognize them instantly. When using the Keirsey and Bates categories we are talking about *temperament* and when using other couplings we are talking about *functional pairs.*

Type and temperament

Keirsey and Bates set out the four temperaments (NT, NF, SJ, SP). The S-N (Sensing – iNtuiting) preference is the first key to determining our temperament. The different ways in which people receive and gather information from the world are crucial if we are to understand where someone is 'coming from'. Without this understanding communication is difficult. If I see a tree and you see a forest each of us believes that s/he is right, and distrust of the other can easily result. As we mentioned earlier, to a Senser a tree is a tree, but to an iNtuitive a tree prompts an image of the bigger system – a forest. Is a glass containing milk half full or half empty? To an iNtuitive (N) the glass is half full as s/he sees the potential and is more optimistic. For the Senser (S), the glass is half empty as s/he focuses on what is actually there – not on what could be there. So the first letter of the temperament is S or N.

The second letter of the temperament is determined by what the first letter is. If it is an N, your preference for gathering information is more abstract and conceptual. Your second most important preference is how you prefer to evaluate the information that you have gathered: more objectively (T or Thinking function) or more subjectively (F or Feeling function). For 'iNtuitives' therefore there are two basic temperament groups, iNtuitive – Feeling (NF) and iNtuitive – Thinking (NT).

If, however, the first letter of your temperament is an S, your preference for gathering information is concrete and specific. The next most important preference therefore is not how you evaluate it but what you do with it. Do you organize it and make judgements about it (J or Judging function)? Or do you continue to take it in and receive more information (P or Perceiving function)? So the two temperament groups for Sensers are: Sensing – Judging (SJ) and Sensing – Perceiving (SP).

Keirsey and Bates give the temperament groups names which most people find far more difficult to remember than the groups themselves. There is no need to remember them (they are taken from Greek mythology) but it is helpful to be able to remember the type combinations. It is worth remembering that the temperaments offer us a handy reference to personality types, but they are something of a short-cut and give an incomplete picture in comparison with using all four preferences.

The SP temperament ('Dionysian')

This temperament is united by its Sensing and Perceiving functions, and what holds it together is greater than the differences within it. It brings together four of the sixteen types, ISTP, ESTP, ISFP and ESFP.

SPs are practical people who are happiest when dealing with concrete problems. The information they receive from the world is practical and realistic (S) and they bring to it spontaneity and flexibility (P). Their Sensing preference grounds them in the reality of the moment and their Perceiving helps them to be open and flexible about the ways of dealing with that reality.

One of the few things that an SP can be sure about is the present moment, now, whereas a long-range plan is almost a contradiction in terms. SPs live for the present moment and they are attracted to careers which deliver immediate and tangible rewards, especially those which involve and demand practical and technical skills. SPs make excellent negotiators and trouble-shooters and are also at their best in crises. When a crisis needs solving the SP can be a genius at creating solutions. Indeed, it is sometimes said that SPs are not above creating crises, because in the solving of them they discover a necessary sense of purpose!

Practicality, resourcefulness, problem-solving requiring 'hands-on' activity . . . these are the hallmarks of the SP. Life with an SP can be a thrill a minute, but this may not be appreciated if his/her partner or children prefer family life based on predictability and orderly structure. SPs are good at practicalities, but they often shy away from the more theoretical or abstract. They will tend to shun intellectual pursuits and prefer those subjects which seem to be practical and immediately rewarding.

They have been described as 'exciting, optimistic, cheerful, light-hearted and full of fun'. They can become easily bored, and like variety; they act on impulse but also have considerable powers of endurance. SPs are process-orientated rather than goal-orientated (goals signify closure, whilst the 'P' in them wants to maintain openness). SPs tend to like the open road, and so they are liable to move on, even if this causes pain to those around them. To them, everything is negotiable.

REALISTIC

process-orientated

FREE SPIRIT

Fun Loving

Impulsive

GOOD
IN
A CRISIS

NEEDS SPACE

ADAPTABLE

PRACTICAL

JOYFUL

FLEXIBLE

ACTION

seeks change & variety

'HANDS ON'

'Let me do something'

The SP temperament

The SJ temperament ('Epimethean')

These are the ISFJ, ESFJ, ISTJ and ESTJ types, and they are bound together by their sense of duty. The information that SJs receive is practical and realistic (S) and they choose to give it structure, and organize it (J).

SJs yearn to belong to meaningful institutions and they become the pillars and backbone of society. They tend to be trustworthy, loyal, helpful, reverent, stabilizing traditionalists. SJs love to organize people, furniture, schedules, timetables, and organizations. Their lives tend to revolve around procedures and it is sometimes said that SJs have a procedure for everything, from making toast to making love!

Many SJs find their fulfilment in administration because of their dependability and their ability to take charge. They can be superb in systems that require precision and organization. They will do what needs to be done today, but sometimes at the expense of what must be done tomorrow.

The home and hearth are the cornerstone of the SJ's relationships. Family roles are clearly defined and family rituals and traditions are preciously maintained and provide a stabilizing factor for family life. Needless to say, to family members who are not SJs, all this can be rather tedious!

SJs feel obligated, in marked contrast to SPs; they warm to structures of authority and hierarchies, rules and regulations and believe that it is important to earn your place and respect within them. They believe that care should be taken, and that they should be forearmed and forewarned against any eventuality. If SPs are carefree then SJs are care*ful*. Tradition is important to SJs, and many assume responsibility within churches and community organizations. In their working lives they are usually found within large organizations where they seek to conserve, maintain and serve. They keep the fabric of our society together and they do the right things at the right time. We would expect most bishops to be SJs!

The NT Temperament ('Promethean')

This temperament brings together the NTs: INTP, ENTP, INTJ and ENTJ. There are thought to be fewer of these in society than of the other temperaments and they are usually in a minority in any

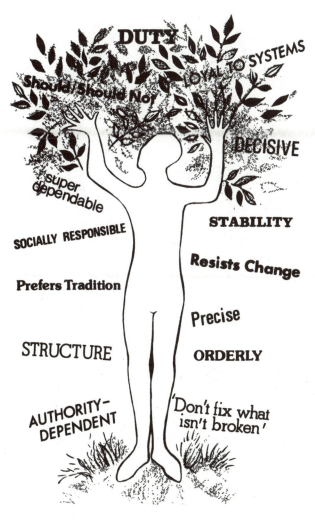

The SJ temperament

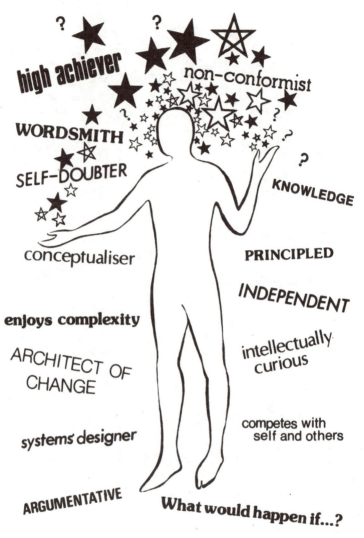

The NT temperament

grouping, whether at work or at leisure, and this can cause them to feel rather isolated at times. What holds them together is a shared concern, perhaps passion would be a better word, for *competence* – they like to do things well under differing circumstances.

The information received by NTs comes in the form of meaning, abstractions and possibilities (N) which is then filtered through their logical, objective, decision-making process (T). The driving force in their continuing quest for competence is to theorise and intellectualize everything. They ask 'Why/Why not?' all the time, and they are enthusiastic pursuers of adventures.

NTs are questioning and challenging of authorities and always seem to be 'testing the system'. In their relentless pursuit of excellence they can be critical of their own, and others', shortcomings. One of their strengths is their ability to see the big picture, their talent is for conceptualization and for planning and developing systems within organizations. They can speak and write clearly and precisely.

NTs are the strategic planners and researchers of the world, though it is possible for them to be so engrossed in their strategies that the day-to-day business is neglected. They tend to intellectualize their feelings and emotions and may be more interested in theorizing about a relationship than nurturing or experiencing it.

The NT is the most critical of all the temperaments and feels the need to be able to do a whole host of tasks, although s/he recognizes, and feels deeply the fact that s/he is not omnicompetent. They can be unduly demanding of those who are around them; they seek competence in themselves and expect to find it in others, especially if they are NTJs. This can lead to a certain amount of withdrawal by others, and so the NT can become rather isolated and this only serves to confirm their view that many of the people around them do not tackle the issues seriously enough. They are in danger of becoming workaholics, they are future-orientated, and they can have difficulty in relating to others, who often find them cool, aloof and 'intellectual'.

The NF Temperament ('Apollonian')

This is the group that contains types INFJ, ENFJ, INFP and ENFP. They look at the world and see the possibilities (N) and then seek to translate these into interpersonal relationships. NFs eat, sleep, breathe, think and love people. They can be seen as 'idealistic do-gooders' who champion various causes, not least those relating to the underdog. Their sensitivity, which is an attractive gift can, however, lead them to personalize any criticism and often feel hurt. The desire for harmony, in oneself and with others, is most important to the NF, as is the quest for personal identity: 'Who am I?' is his/her haunting question.

NFs have a great capacity for working with people and for encouraging and enabling others to give their best. They are able to affirm others freely and easily, and they have a strong desire to be of help. They are positive, affirming idealists, and tend to be liked by other people – so much so, in fact, that sometimes people may find it difficult to disagree with them. As they have a great dislike of conflict they may find it hard to be firm supervisors and they seek to avoid confrontational disagreements.

Whilst the other temperaments can be summed up in just one or two words such as 'freedom' (SPs), 'duty' (SJs) and 'competence' (NTs), it is more difficult to summarize the NFs – perhaps 'being' is the nearest. It has been said that the NF's truest self is the self in search of itself! His/her purpose in life is to have a purpose in life. NFs need to have feedback, they need to know that their contribution to the job, the company, the family or the discussion is valued. Without a sense of meaning the NFs are rootless, anxious and insecure.

Genuineness, authenticity, integrity – these are the hallmarks of the NF temperament. NFs want to improve the world, be of significance and accepted as people who have something to offer. NFs are strong on relationships, they are sensitive to body language, keen communicators and they can have quite a sense of the dramatic. They give of themselves and receive from others – this is what sustains them, and they often cannot understand why everyone else is not also caught up in this search for meaning and this sharing of pain and joy.

Within the family they have been described as teddy bears, because their own need to give and receive affection and avoid conflict, may reduce their relationships to 'a hug a day to keep the problems away' – but, of course, there is more to relationships than hugs.

NFs are to be found in all the caring professions, in teaching (more in schools than in universities) and in the arts – in the theatre, for example, where they can become the person portrayed

very sensitive to conflict

GOOD INTER-PERSONAL SKILLS

searches for self

SUPPORTIVE
OF OTHERS

sympathetic

GOOD AT
RELATIONSHIPS

vivid imagination

needs encouragement

mysterious

'has integrity'

AUTONOMOUS

CO-OPERATIVE

an encourager

sees possibilities in people

BECOMING

The NF temperament

– or as novelists, where they can weave a whole web of relationships and explore the meanings of life.

Needing each other

There is a Yorkshire phrase 'There's nowt so queer as folk', which is just another way of expressing astonishment at the rich diversity of personality types that we see around us. All different, and yet with sufficient common strands for us to be able to recognize that certain types seem to belong together. There is a strange tension in groups of people which seems to need opposites, contrasts or complementarities in order to maintain the equilibrium of our social fabric. We need each other, and even people we find difficult to understand or appreciate have an important role to play in ensuring that all the gifts are shared out, that all the skills are available, and that each one of us has a special place and part to play in the overall scheme of things.

In their highly readable book *Type Talk* Otto Kroeger and Janet Thuesen give a clear illustration of different temperaments enjoying an afternoon's leisure together:

> We have a swimming pool so we entertain a lot in the summer. Our SP guests always grab all the pool toys, head right for the water, and invent a new game. The NFs sprawl on the lounge chairs and talk earnestly about life and people. The NTs dangle their feet in the water, rib each other, and critique the issues and people in their professions. And the SJs always, always find some work to do, like hanging up towels, husking corn, scrubbing the grill, or pulling weeds from the garden.[2]

Part Two

6 | People Living Together

Families can be a source of joy and fulfilment, they can also be seedbeds of pain, frustration and misunderstanding. Living with other people is not easy, and as families grow in size so the possibilities for misunderstanding also grow. For two people living together, there is one relationship to work at. For three people living together, there are three relationships. Four people in a family provide six different relationships and five people provide ten. [To discover the number of different relationships the formula is: the number of people in the group multiplied by the number of people minus one, divided by two.]

Understanding our own type should mean that we now appreciate some of the things that appeal to us and some of the things that don't; we should also now be able to understand why we find some things easier to cope with than others, and why we prefer certain situations to others. Understanding our own type has opened up to us a whole range of insights and possibilities, helped us to come to terms with some of our limitations and to appreciate some of our gifts. We now need to be able to do the same sort of exercise for the people with whom we live.

If we can begin to understand what sort of situations they find difficult, what they have to offer, and how these relate to our own personality preferences, then perhaps we might understand better some of the disruptions and stresses that occur, day by day, to the relationships in which we are involved. A good case could be argued to suggest that clergy should provide a Myers Briggs exercise as a normal part of their marriage preparation with couples who come to them to arrange their weddings. It would be an enormous help to people, starting out on married life, if they had some understanding of the areas in which they might inevitably conflict, or fail to appreciate the needs of the other.

A newly-wed couple were driving off on their honeymoon. The wedding had been a huge success, friends from all over had gathered together and the reception had been informal, extremely joyful and could hardly have been bettered. However, after about an hour in the car Mary began to grow uncomfortable, and she couldn't quite understand why. Time passed, and it became obvious to her that something was wrong; eventually she tackled Ian, and wanted to know what had upset him. He was astonished by the question and wondered what on earth had got into her. She explained that they had hardly spoken since they set off, and that he seemed distant – was he now regretting the whole thing? No, he had never felt better, he replied; he was driving along feeling at total peace with himself and the world. What was not clear to Mary was that Ian was basically an Introvert, and this particular morning he was utterly content and totally at home in his own private world. During the time when they were courting, and especially in all the preparations for the wedding, he had been very extravert – talking to this person and that, arranging one thing after another, and ensuring that Mary was happy with all the arrangements. Now all those people had gone home, and he and Mary were alone at last, he no longer had to operate in his less-preferred mode. It was only several years later, when they had both gone on a Myers Briggs Workshop that Mary suddenly remembered this incident and realized what had been happening.

It was one of Isabel Briggs Myers' stated hopes that parents might understand their children better, by understanding type, and refrain from trying to impose upon them their own ways of looking at things, their own hopes and fears, and their own ideas about the future and possible careers, friends or partners. What pain could be avoided if parents were able to honour their children's type! As a university chaplain several years ago, I was constantly meeting students (usually about half way through their second year) who felt that they were on the wrong course. So many of them told me that they were unsure of what to do when they were thinking about university, but that their parents had wanted them to do a certain course and so they had obliged, but now they knew that this was not what they wanted to do, and they resented the fact that they felt they had been pressurized into starting it. Similarly, I will never forget (nor will I be allowed to) the fact that I persuaded my daughter Kate at a very young age that it would be silly to learn to play the flute as everyone else seemed to be playing it, why not do something different and learn to play the saxophone, which she duly did. To this day I have a frustrated flautist for a daughter, and I cringe with shame when I recall the incident.

In looking at how we relate to the people we live with, we need to realize that certain reactions are likely when, for example, Introverts relate to Introverts, or Sensers relate to iNtuitives, Judgers relate to Judgers, or Thinkers relate to Feelers. Each pair of relationships will have certain positive dynamics, but each will also throw up some problems. Our ability to recognize and deal with the outcome of these 'meetings of type' will, to a very large extent, determine the quality of our relationships.

Extraverts relating to Extraverts

On the positive side, it obviously helps when both share the same environment to which they relate and are enthused or energized by. This contrasts with Introverts who may very well not share the same environment as others. Extraverts will be focusing on people, situations and events, and because this has been their preference over the years, they will both have developed certain skills and experience in dealing with this environment. They will also recognize and understand how the other person goes about their own process of relating. Extraverts may be able to express their love more openly, and may be good at recognizing and meeting the needs of the other.

Both people may have broad interests and may share and enjoy a wide variety of social contacts. They will tend to have an active approach to life, and since Extraverts get their batteries charged by extraverting, they will be able to support and energize each other. Extraverts tend to communicate a lot, and are concerned to be constantly relating. They may both be great talkers, and use the telephone a great deal.

Extraverts are usually able to give affirmation to each other each day, they both need to be affirmed by others, especially by *the* other. They will recognize the process of 'thinking out loud', and there will not be much of a hidden agenda, as Extraverts tend to like to have everything out in the open. There may be occasional eruptions, but they tend to be short-lived, even if dramatic!

On the debit side, there can be too much focusing on the external world and not enough introversion; this will therefore mean that their auxiliary functions remain undeveloped (Extraverts use their dominant function for extraversion and their auxiliary is introverted). There is always the danger that when one of them wants to be 'private', the other will not understand that need and may try to deny it to them or become jealous of it.

Two Extraverts living together may become so involved in outside issues – their work, their church or other organizations – that they may have difficulty allotting enough time and space for themselves or for each other; and they may be so busy doing or talking that they fail to listen to the other. Since Extraverts tend to be directive or assertive, there may be a struggle for the limelight, and there may well be a whole variety of power struggles. Since they tend to act first and then think, and learn by trial and error, Extravert relationships are likely to contain a number of mistakes, and these can eventually mount up and be quite burdensome.

There is a danger that Extraverts burn out from too much talking and doing; they need to relax and be quiet, even though they may not recognize or admit this need. A constant preoccupation with the external world may lead to insufficient reflection and thinking, and so there is always the danger that Extravert relationships have too little intellectual content, and thus they can appear shallow to Introverts. In later life, as preferences become more mature or developed, there is then the danger that one partner may 'outgrow' the other, and so it is important that reflective and intellectual elements are built into the relationship from early on.

Introverts relating to Introverts

As Introverts, both people will have great need for privacy and space and are likely to give each other a considerable amount of psychological distance; both prefer to concentrate upon their inner world of concepts and ideas and, of course, they may have widely differing worlds which energize them. Introverts together are quite content for there to be times of quiet; they are not in need of constant conversation – something which Extraverts find difficult to understand. Introverts are able to sustain long and deep one-to-one relationships, and they are able to understand each other, and their respective needs, without making constant reference to what is happening. When they do talk, they prefer to have in-depth conversations about something which they both believe to be important.

If one, or both, of the Introverts has to be out at work 'extraverting', they will need time and space when they get home to relax and re-charge their batteries, and they are likely to find this relatively easy when living with another Introvert.

Problems that Introverts face tend to stem from the conflict between their need to relate to the outer world and their preference for their inner world. Two Introverts may be facing the same outer world but may have very different inner worlds, and there can be real difficulties in communicating across that gap. They may both have difficulties in sending and receiving signals to and from each other. Because they don't like asking for information, they tend not to give information unless asked, and yet when asked, they may feel uncomfortable answering! Introverts also have a tendency to think that they have given more information than they actually have.

When living together, Introverts may have problems in resolving who is to take the initiative in various ventures: Who, for instance, decides on where to go for holidays, and who books? Who decides whether to ask friends round for the evening? (Do we actually *want* to have friends round anyway?) There are many occasions when at least one of them must extravert, but then who decides on this?

Another problem that Introverts might easily experience is that of checking against reality some of their values or their learned responses to various situations. As a result of their preference for internalizing, there is less likelihood that Introverts 'put out for inspection' their views or attitudes, and so, if they are wrong or misplaced, there is less likelihood that experience will show this and allow them to modify them.

Two Introverts living together must ensure that they communicate, and that they have enough time together when they share common experiences. They also have to ensure that they know how to pick up enough clues so as to know how the other is feeling or thinking – and that means focusing on the external world, which they prefer not to do. There is also the danger that neither of them sufficiently exercises their auxiliary, which is the function through which they relate to the external world and which consequently can make their extraverting rather abrupt or clumsy.

Extraverts and Introverts relating to each other

An Extravert and an Introvert living together can provide a good balance between talking and listening in a way that suits both preferences: Extraverts love having someone to talk to and Introverts are good listeners. An Extravert was asked what he did to ensure that he had a good date when meeting a girl for the first time. He was surprised by the question and replied 'I just turn up!' – whether or not the date turned out equally as well if the girl was also an Extravert was never revealed!

Extraverts often choose Introverts for partners, as they provide them with a balance of peace and quiet, and similarly, an Extravert can provide vitality and a sense of outgoing for an Introvert. Extraverts like initiating and leading, and Introverts prefer to follow. Working well together, this partnership can enjoy both breadth and depth. If the Extravert is male and the Introvert is female, this fits the sexual stereotype of our society and helps ease social relationships; if it is the other way round, society finds it more difficult, and the women are sometimes seen as being 'pushy' and the men as being 'hen–pecked', such observations may or may not be correct.

Extraverts and Introverts often provide good company for each other, opposites very often do attract. The Extravert can help to provide a reality check for the Introvert, whilst the Introvert can provide some depth and objectivity for the Extravert. They can both be a great help to the other in developing their auxiliaries.

Problems can arise though when Extraverts talk too much for their Introvert partners or companions, or when Introverts want more privacy and quiet than the Extraverts are prepared to tolerate; there is always a danger that one (or both) remains unfulfilled. They need to recognize that they each re-charge their batteries in different ways, and Introverts need to realize that Extraverts need more affirmation than they do.

Introverts tend to think things through on their own, and then come up with their views. They may be reluctant to change their minds on something which they have pondered over for a long time. This is difficult for Extraverts to understand, for they tend to express their views and preferences early, before they have given them overmuch thought. The reluctance of Introverts to change their mind can be interpreted by Extraverts as stubbornness, and the extra pressure that they then exert can lead to Introverts becoming even more determined, for they feel that something which is important to them has come under threat.

Extraverts can overwhelm Introverts with too much talk, and can exasperate them by saying the same thing three times over but in different words. The Introvert is inclined to tell them that they heard them the first time! Conversely, because Introverts ponder things internally, they can often think that they have communicated something when they haven't; they may never have mentioned it at all, only thought that they had, or they may have mentioned it once without registering that it had not been picked up by the Extravert. Extraverts can also feel 'left out' of the thinking process: they like to share their thinking, explore ideas and fine-tune or completely alter their conclusions. Introverts come up with the finished goods and can unwittingly hurt the Extravert who feels excluded and discounted.

Extraverts can deny Introverts sufficient time to process their thoughts and expect quick, provisional answers, whereas Introverts tend to shy away from hasty or provisional judgements. Also, because Extraverts tend to think aloud, they may well come up with ideas or views which upset Introverts, who then tend to duck away into their shell and don't hear later views or ideas expressed by the Extraverts which may be modifications of the original ideas. It might be a good idea for Introverts to ask 'Is that your considered opinion, or are you just thinking aloud?' – a lot of misunderstanding could then be avoided!

An Introverted American man was driving through central London. It was taking all his concentration, and being an NT as well he was particularly concerned to do it well. It didn't leave a great deal of spare capacity for him to engage in conversation, but for his Extraverted partner London traffic was no great problem and she had a seemingly limitless amount of time and space. Just when he was negotiating Hyde Park Corner his partner asked 'Where do you think our relationship is going?'!

Judy Provost, the director of Personal Counselling at Rollins College, Winter Park, Florida has drawn attention to the different ways in which types have disagreements[1]. Extraverts, according to Judy Provost, tend to want to sort the problems out immediately whereas Introverts prefer to withdraw until they understand what is happening. If they confront the problem now, the Introvert will probably lose the argument because they are confused, and may well start it up again later when they have clarified things in their mind. If there is a delay in sorting it out, then the Extravert gets frustrated and will tend to try and corner the Introvert and insist on thrashing it out now. Provost suggests that the best way forward is for the Extravert to give the Introvert some warning – for example: 'I'm having a problem with this, can we talk about it later?' – thus giving the Introvert time, and the Introvert can help in this process by agreeing, and suggesting that they come back to it in an hour or so.

Sensers relating to Sensers

When Sensers share their lives, they are likely to be able to do lots of practical work within the home, as both will enjoy 'hands on' experiences. It is likely that their home will be neat and tidy, things will be put away, breakages will be attended to and the garden will be trim. They will share an interest in doing things, and going places, and will probably have a mutual interest in sport, travel, music or the theatre. Their lives will be quite busy, very likely, and they will probably be activists of one sort or another. Sensers are aware of their bodies and take care of them.

On the negative side, there is always the danger that they get stuck in routines and prefer not to use or develop their imagination in a whole range of imaginative ways. When things are going wrong for Sensers, they tend to be rather pessimistic, and are not on the look-out for possibilities and breakthroughs. They live very much in the here and now, and their present experiences are all-important. They are less likely than other types to seek counselling if a relationship breaks down.

iNtuitives relating to iNtuitives

For iNtuitive types variety is the spice of life, and so there is likely to be a rich diversity in these relationships. They will be full of ideas and possibilities and the future will be very important to them – so much so that the present will hardly be noticed at times. There may well be untidiness around the home, especially if one, or both, is also a Perceiver. Household jobs may remain undone, and new pieces of machinery may remain a mystery until one of them reads the instructions; it may take months (or years) to understand the washing machine programmes! They can help one another in problem-solving, and are likely to bounce up relatively quickly after any setbacks. They will be able to communicate quite quickly with each other; they may not even have to finish their sentences! They are likely to place a high value on education, seeing it as an important investment in the future, and may enjoy working with complex situations and theorizing about them. Both will tend to work on impulse, and there will be times of great and sustained endeavour, and also times of relative quiet when not a great deal seems to be happening.

Because they are both future-orientated, two iNtuitives can fail to deal with present issues and problems, and they can postpone or avoid those things which they prefer not to address. They can fail to notice what is in their cupboards, and easily duplicate purchases. As neither of them is too keen on details, there is always a danger that they jump to conclusions, and can end up making decisions which they live to regret. One reason why iNtuitives often jump to conclusions is that they have an inbuilt problem in reaching decisions as there are always other possibilities to explore – and this tendency is compounded if one or both of them is also a Perceiver.

When there is strain on the relationship, iNtuitives are likely not to acknowledge it, preferring to transfer their thoughts into the future, to a time when the problems won't exist. They may therefore endure an unsatisfying relationship, eventually becoming resigned to being unfulfilled by it.

Sensers and iNtuitives relating to each other

At their best iNtuitives can generate great new ideas which Sensers are able to make happen, and they are able to complement each other in a most stimulating and mutually satisfying manner. When things are not working well though, the Senser can be irritated beyond measure by the iNtuitive's lack of interest in putting things right, mending the lamp or decorating the bedroom, and the Senser can appear to the iNtuitive as being someone who is constantly nagging or pointing out problems and faults!

Sensers are often good homemakers, and can be appreciated for that by iNtuitives who like an attractive home base but often do very little about establishing it. On the other hand, the Senser can appreciate the iNtuitive's ability not to get bogged down by practical problems and their gift of being able to have bright new ideas. INtuitive partners are also good to be with because they tend not to notice the greying hair, the additional pounds or extra wrinkles – although they can also be a source of despair by having little sense of dress, and caring little about such an omission!

Sensers can help the iNtuitives to enjoy the here and now, and iNtuitives can help Sensers to look forward to the future. It has been said that an iNtuitive–Senser relationship provides the balance between the dream and the chequebook!

INtuitive types may not notice noise levels, or smells . . . and this can be difficult for Sensers, whereas Sensers may not always appreciate how important dreams and hopes for the future are to iNtuitives, and they can trample on their sensitivities without realizing it.

Communication can be quite a problem between the two, and if mutual respect breaks down then Sensers can be interpreted as being rather dull and boring and iNtuitives can be written off as intellectual snobs, daydreamers or just plain eccentrics. When it comes to disagreements, there are likely to be problems with the content of the argument rather than with the process. INtuitive types want to explore the patterns of the relationship, what it means and where it is going, and they see things in broad terms. Sensers, however, want to deal with specifics and argue about 'facts'. INtuitives think that Sensers are nit-picking and they, in turn, think that iNtuitives read far too much into things. If there is a healthy respect between the two then there can be a complementary array of gifts which is both powerful and practical.

Dorothy, a Senser is married to Martin an iNtuitive. A bedroom curtain rail had collapsed and Martin, who possessed no DIY tools whatsoever, chose not to notice this until Dorothy could stand it no longer and tackled him about getting it put right. On closer inspection they discovered that plaster had come off the wall and that they couldn't just screw the rail back up. This provided Martin with an interesting problem which he could put his mind to, and he came up with the bright idea of plugging the gaps with polyfilla and inserting screws into it just before it set so that they would be held securely. Satisfied with this solution, he explained it to Dorothy, who got out the step ladder and put up the curtain rail accordingly!

Thinkers relating to Thinkers

Thinkers living together will probably enjoy analysing things, and will easily agree upon logical structures. They will be capable of tackling issues which need to be tackled, and they will understand that feelings are very often expressed as thoughts. They will tell the truth as they see it and not expect to hurt the other, nor are they likely to feel hurt by what is said to them. They are very often task-orientated, and enjoy accomplishing things. Thinkers can have very deep and loving relationships, but these may not be expressed openly – in fact they may well fight shy of overt demonstrations of affection. They will have a high respect for the sense and ability of the other.

On the debit side, both may have difficulty in being in touch with their emotions and expressing feelings, and this can be hurtful to others at times. They are unable to help each other in this area, and consequently the most likely expression of feeling, when it does occur, is that of anger. Although they may have worked their lives out in a very logical way, they are sometimes at a loss to know how to handle situations when people behave illogically. Not only are they unable to provide the feelings that the other may at times need, they are also unable to recognize or express their own emotional needs. Thinkers in relationships need to learn how to give positive reinforcements to the other and find ways of expressing the reality of their caring. They tend to be a lot stronger on solving problems and being critical than in affirming people and situations.

Feelers relating to Feelers

Relationships between Feelers are characterized by harmony, as both desire this for the other and for him/herself. They will each be sensitive to how the other feels and aware of what might cause pain or difficulty. They will probably share similar values, and this will minimize the opportunities for conflict. The relationship will be of very great importance to them both, and take precedence over other claims upon their time and thoughts. (This is in contrast to relationships between Thinkers where, very often, the relationship, although important, is secondary to other concerns.)

There is likely to be an open expresson of feeling and affection, and because they both work best in a secure and safe environment, they will endeavour to ensure that they provide it. They will be good at 'reading each other's thoughts' and there will be easy and relaxed communication between them – although Extraverted Perceivers (who introvert their Feeling) and Introverted Feelers may find difficulty in expressing what is important to each other.

Feelers are not particularly good at being tough when the occasion demands it, neither is objectivity their strongest point. They tend to personalize and particularize almost everything, and so the slightest criticism can be taken very seriously and pondered over, and cause considerable pain. They will almost certainly have difficulty in expressing anger, and will tend to internalize and subdue it – but it may well break out at some later stage, and the strength and depth of it then may bear little relation to the event which triggered it off.

There will be strong temptations to try and manipulate the other, and guilt is never far from the surface when Feelers are around! They can be remarkably stubborn when their values are challenged, and they may have real difficulties in expressing themselves logically when required to defend their position. Feelers have a tendency to see things in black-and-white terms (their Thinking function is not so well developed) and this can sometimes lead them into trouble when situations do not develop or turn out as they were expecting.

Relationships between Feelers can be very affectionate, affirming and welcoming, but when things are under strain they can be so afraid of hurting each other (or of being hurt) that honesty and openness can be avoided. There will always be a danger of one (or both) of them being smothered.

Thinkers and Feelers relating to each other

Thinkers and Feelers can offer each other complementarity: the Thinker bringing some objectivity into the home and the Feeler providing the personal awareness and tenderness. The Thinker can do some of the 'tough' things, and the Feeler can be persuasive, conciliatory or enthusiastic, depending upon the situation.

More negatively, the Feeler may not always appreciate the logical and 'cool' approach of the Thinker, who may, in turn, experience the Feeler as being altogether too gushy and sentimental. There will be a fine balance to be reached between the one's desire for harmony and the other's capacity for criticism. The Feeler may not receive sufficient affirmation from the Thinker, who may well belittle his/her need for it, and there may be a tendency for the Feeler to assume the responsibility for any problems or failures in the relationship – and the Thinker will let him/her!

When the relationship works well, Thinkers and Feelers provide a good balance to each other, but when problems arise there is the possibility of the Thinker making a critical comment, which the Feeler then takes personally, feels hurt about and expresses in an emotional way. The Thinker cannot cope with emotional outbursts and therefore withdraws and becomes even more analytical!

When they argue, the Feeler expresses his or her feelings, and wishes the Thinker to do so as well, when s/he then responds with a thought rather than a feeling this is interpreted as a cop-out! If the Thinker begins the argument, an idea is expressed, if this is met with an emotion rather than with another idea then the Thinker dismisses the response as irrelevant. A way through this impasse is for them each to express their point of view, and then try and put themselves in the other's shoes and say, 'If I were you, I would want to put it this way . . .'.

Perceivers relating to Perceivers

This is likely to be a relaxed, casual and non-judgemental relationship. They will communicate easily, and have lots of ideas and new information to share with each other. It will almost certainly be a relationship with plenty of fun and spontaneity, and it could be very creative. Both will be able to adapt to changing situations and circumstances quite well, and they are likely to be forgiving and tolerant of each other, and of other people.

However, they are likely to have problems with time and with planning. There will be a tendency to take too many things on board and perhaps not finish all that they have promised to do;

the temptation to be over-committed may leave other people slightly exasperated. Their home may well become overcrowded and untidy, and there will always be the problem of losing things, and not leaving enough time to find them. This can be relatively harmless when it relates to pieces of clothing, but can be stressful if it concerns the air-tickets to the holiday destination! There is likely to be an atmosphere of relaxed well-being punctuated by spurts of last-minute panic. Two Perceivers together may well delay taking important decisions, and have decisions imposed upon them by others instead. Similarly, they may not be very good at organizing holidays, time-off together, or important family events. Small decisions very often demand major effort, and quite often nothing gets done!

Judgers relating to Judgers

These relationships achieve a great deal: things are planned well, organized and, if possible, delegated. Few things are left to chance, and people around them who are not Judgers can feel over-organized, or overwhelmed even. Both people work well in structured situations, and it is likely that they have worked out endless systems to ensure the smooth running of the home. They will rely upon each other a great deal and know that the other is reliable.

Judgers enjoy making decisions, and both will be looking for 'closure' in as many situations as possible. There is always the possibility therefore that decisions are made too quickly – before all the possible alternatives have been explored or all the information considered. They can also over-simplify complex issues; sometimes this is helpful, but it can be a dangerous route to follow. They can become very rigid in their opinions and lifestyle, and may miss a lot by not allowing themselves to be spontaneous and flexible. Commitment to work may mean that much enjoyment is foregone and a great deal of pleasure missed. As parents, Judgers may be too strict with their children, and develop too many expectations of themselves, their partners and their family; this can be very burdensome.

By planning and structuring their lives Judgers can create time and space to do a great many things, and their lives can be full and interesting. They can, however, get into power struggles over who will make the decisions – when this happens they may make a plan to sort out who makes what decisions in which particular areas!

Perceivers and Judgers relating to each other

They can complement each other by one providing the perceiving input and the other making decisions. The Perceivers can help restrain the Judgers from becoming too rigid and too serious, and in turn, the Judgers can help Perceivers from being too loose and disorganized, and from making too many promises and commitments. At its best, this combination can combine work and play in a most creative way, but when it goes wrong it can become a negative cycle in which the Judger may try to persuade the Perceiver to do something, and if they resist then the pressure mounts and the resistance grows stronger!

The Perceiver's desire to save and collect things (and leave them around) can irritate the Judger beyond measure; in turn, the Judger's desire to clear things up and throw things out can hurt or frustrate the Perceiver. They may have difficulty in communicating where decisions are concerned: the Judger thinking that things have been decided – before they have, and the Perceiver thinking that they haven't been decided – after they have!

Problems can arise from the tendency of Judgers to apply pressure on others to make them more like themselves. Whilst Perceivers are happy for people to be different, Judgers aren't! Tensions can also arise when Judgers endeavour to ensure that plans are prepared well in advance and Perceivers manage to keep options open. Judgers experience stress until a decision is made, then they can relax; meanwhile Perceivers experience stress if they are called upon to make a decision.

This is the axis on which differences are probably most apparent, and on which they can cause greater misunderstanding.

One couple came to grief when the Perceiving partner complained that they were always having to do things 'his way'; 'he' was amazed by such an accusation and said that he was diligent in trying to ensure that he 'heard' what his wife was saying. What he hadn't taken into consideration was that when a Perceiver says that something is a good idea, what they actually mean is that it is one good idea amongst many others. It is not stating a wish, but rather it is an opinion expressed on a wide canvas. In this particular case, the husband, anxious to please, had acted on his wife's views, but he hadn't heard what she wasn't saying!

When it comes to arguments, Judgers try to insist that decisions are made there and then, whereas Perceivers want to avoid making a commitment. Sometimes, a Perceiver will agree to something to placate his/her partner, but being a Perceiver s/he never sees a decision as being final, so s/he may very well change his/her mind later! A better way of resolving problems is for the Judger to present the argument to his/her partner as contrasting options, and then ask him/her what the pros and cons are on each side; Perceivers are much more likely to respond to that than being presented with an ultimatum or a single argument.

An overview

Differences in personality type between partners can lead to confusion and friction, but this can be handled positively if you are able to understand how and why the misunderstandings have arisen. We are sometimes asked if there is a 'right' combination of letters which will ensure that relationships last, and the answer is an unequivocal '*No!*' Relationships grow and depend upon mutual acceptance, affirmation and understanding, and if these are present then any combination of letters, or different types, can form a lasting relationship. Different types bring different gifts to a relationship, and they will also bring their own specific difficulties, their less-preferred options. If you can recognize and accept these, then there is no reason why different types should not have deep and lasting relationships. Quite a lot of work is being done in this area, and the latest research suggests that most couples seem to find partners who are similar to them on two or three preferences; but that really tells us very little, and certainly has no comment to make upon the quality of the relationships.

In her book *Gifts Differing* Isabel Briggs Myers had a section: 'Type and Marriage' and she concluded:

'In any marriage a type difference may at times produce an outright conflict between opposite points of view. When this happens, the partners have a choice. One or both can assume that it is wrong of the other to be different – and be righteously indignant, which diminishes the partner. They can assume that it is wrong of themselves to be different – and be depressed, which is self-diminishing. Or they can acknowledge that each is *justifiably* and *interestingly* different from the other – and be amused. Their amusement may be warm or detached, wry or tender, according to their types, but it will help in working out the situation and keeping intact each partner's dignity and the precious fabric of their marriage.'[2]

At a time when an increasing number of relationships seem to be breaking down as a result of stresses of one kind or another, an understanding of type can be a considerable help in recognizing some of the unspoken things that are happening. It can help us to appreciate differences, and it can prevent unnecessary accusations being made against others or against ourselves. Understanding differences in type cannot guarantee perfect partnerships, but it can certainly shed light on, and enhance, the way in which we communicate within relationships.

$\boxed{7}$ Teams Working Together

A great deal of life is spent at work, and for most people, being at work means being with other people. The Myers Briggs Type Indicator can be a useful tool in helping you understand what is happening in the dynamics of your work situation. It can offer a theoretical framework within which to address issues such as personality conflict, motivation and frustration in a way which is neither pejorative nor judgemental, and which can move the discussion forward from the potentially hazardous quagmire of specific individuals and what we like or don't like about them. An increasing number of organizations are now using the Indicator in programmes of staff training and development, alongside a battery of other tests, and it is often used when there are breakdowns in communication or confidence within working groups.

In Chapter 5 we dealt with the mutual usefulness of opposite types; discussed how no one person has all the gifts and skills, and how a person who may be marvellous at seeing the 'big picture' may have difficulties with small detail; how people who are extremely logical may not be sufficiently sensitive to the needs of the people around them. We have noted how some people prefer to keep all their options open until the very last minute, whereas others like to reach conclusions at the earliest possible moment, and we have seen that some people think before they speak whilst some others may use the very process of speaking as a means of assembling their thoughts. The preferences which people express, and which serve to differentiate them from others are also, inevitably, taken into their working environments, and in Chapter 2 we gave some examples of how different preferences often show themselves in work situations.

It is a helpful exercise to work out the different types in a particular team situation, and then to see where the probable strengths and weaknesses of that team might emerge. Working with a small group of people who were setting up a community centre/resource centre and drop-in coffee bar in a northern city, revealed that they were all strongly iNtuative. This came as no surprise, for it was a visionary concept, but it was necessary to explore with them who was going to provide the essential concern for detail which a Senser would regard as basic, but which might well prove to be tedious and irksome for an iNtuitive type.

In a similar way, it is possible to envisage situations where, say, too many Perceivers in a group might mean that decisions were hardly ever made; too many Judgers could mean that decisions were made rather too hastily, without sufficient thought being given to other alternatives. When forming teams, or working groups, there is always a temptation to bring together people like ourselves, rather than ensuring that a wide range of type and temperament is considered. We take it as common sense, when building a house, to recognize that we will need builders, electricians, plumbers, joiners and plasterers – that is, people with specific skills for specific tasks. Is it all that different to recognize that we will need differing personality types if working teams are to function effectively and efficiently together?

Extraverts prefer to operate in the external world: they are action-orientated; Introverts prefer the inner world of ideas and concepts. Sensing – Feeling types (SFs) are interested in facts and details, and will tend to interpret these from a personal or human perspective; Sensing – Thinking types (STs), who are also interested in facts and details will prefer to analyse them impersonally – in the example I gave earlier, what the small group of people needed was to invite an SF to join them in their planning.

Those who combine iNtuition with Feeling (NFs) are interested in possibilities, particularly as they affect people; they will be concerned to explore new truths and ideas, and may often prefer to do this alongside other people (especially if they are also Extravert). People combining iNtuition with Thinking (NTs) share this concern for the future and for possibilities, but they will be inclined to analyse them impersonally, and may well have a leaning for theoretical and technical processes.

Perceivers are flexible, open to new ideas, very adaptable and perhaps reluctant to reach decisions, whereas Judgers are only too ready to make decisions. Judgers also tend to be orderly, decisive and with clear ideas about what needs to be done, and the ways in which it should be done.

Already, in these simple descriptions, you may be able to recognize situations or people in your own work situation. Add to these, the need that Feelers have for harmony, and their dislike of taking any decisions which may hurt or annoy people, and the Thinkers' ability for making decisions without realizing what they are doing to the people around them, and we have all the ingredients for workplace frustration and misunderstanding!

By understanding type and temperament it is possible to observe or identify what it is that different people appreciate and what it is that annoys them – and of course, we include ourselves in this process!

INtuitive – Thinkers (NTs) like to be appreciated, above all, for their competence, their ideas and capabilities. They expect things to be done well, and so are not very likely to affirm colleagues who are getting on with their jobs, and they can therefore appear to be unappreciative and rather remote and aloof. They will be irritated by incompetence, and by anything that does not appear to be logical. INtuitive – Feelers (NFs) on the other hand, like to be affirmed by others; they like to think that they have a specific, personal contribution to make and they like to be appreciated not only for their ideas and their work, but also for themselves, as people. What they find difficult to cope with is being treated impersonally, the feeling that they are being taken for granted. They appreciate greatly the small gift or gesture when they have worked particularly well or beyond the call of duty, whereas the NT only wants their competence to be noted – that is reward in itself, and a bunch of flowers or small gift might be extremely embarrassing to them.

The Sensing – Judging temperament (SJs) are concerned with accuracy, dependability and thoroughness. They want to be appreciated for their loyalty and devotion to duty, hardwork and conscientiousness, but may be rather diffident about expressing such a need and may well conceal their pleasure when they are praised or thanked. What they find irritating and burdensome are things like deadlines not being met, people not keeping to their word or not using standard and recognized procedures. They do not like brinksmanship, whether in themselves or in others, and resent prima donnas.

Sensing-Perceivers (SPs) tend to like to be appreciated for their flair, their panache, their responsiveness to situations, their willingness to take risks, and their bravado and sense of timing. They are action-orientated people and like to be appreciated for their ability to enjoy and make the most of the present situation. When things are difficult, they maintain the equilibrium and keep people happy until the iNtuitives come up with some bright ideas to sort things out! What they do not like is having to conform, and being told what to do. They are individualists, and like to be appreciated for what they are, and not put into some sort of predetermined mould.

It ought to be possible now to begin to place yourself and others within a work situation, and to realize that, however well or otherwise the actual job is done, the responses from others that are desired or disliked will be different for different people. The skill of the team leader is in being able to respond to the members of the team in an appropriate manner. The same words of encouragement or appreciation which are given to one person may not be at all apposite when given to another, similarly, critical words which one person takes on board in the manner in which you intended may keep another person awake all night in distress.

It is a good exercise to get the members of a team together, and to ask them to make a list of what they think their strengths are as a work group. They may well come to the conclusion that they are nicely balanced, with a good blend of type and temperament, or they may be aware that they are lacking in certain areas but strong in others. What makes for strength in a work situation will obviously change with the nature of the work: marriage guidance teams will want a combination of types different from a group of car salesmen; accountants will tend to differ in their teams' needs from theatre designers, and a group of clergy may differ from furniture removal teams.

Having reflected upon your team's strengths, the next step is then to try and identify what the weaknesses are. In which areas is it under-represented? Does the team include the types and temperaments which 'match' the needs or objectives of the organization? This may well be the occasion when you can also begin to explore how team members experience difficulties in communicating with each other, and in understanding why this should be so. The final exercise would then be to assist the team to explore ways in which each member might contribute to the task of solving the problem that corporately faces the team, and in identifying the specific and unique contribution that each member has to offer to the others.

Coping with the idiosyncrasies of type

The ideas in this section draw heavily upon a series of articles under the general title of 'The Manager's Toolbox' which appeared in some issues of *The Type Reporter* a few years ago[1]. The articles looked at the specific problems thrown up by each preference, and gave hints on how they might be addressed. In the view of the authors, most problems in workplaces stemmed from the tension between Judgers and Perceivers, and so we will start with them. The catchy sub-titles are taken directly from the articles.

How to keep Js from jumping to conclusions

1. Give them new information in advance so that they can spend time alone thinking about it

Judgers (Js) very often find it difficult to change their minds once they have come to a decision; similarly, they find it difficult to change written work once they have committed themselves to paper. They can sometimes become quite confrontational if it is suggested that changes should be made, and so there is value in giving them time to think over any alterations when they are alone and away from the pressures of the situation. This may mean writing a memo, or making suggestions written onto the text, but give them time and space to reflect, and to re-assemble their thoughts; when they have that, they may well take the suggestions on board and come up with a new decision!

2. Acknowledge the value of their judgements beneath the annoying style

Judgers have a tendency to leap to hasty conclusions in a manner which can be extremely irritating. Sometimes they make their judgements on the flimsiest of evidence – but there may well be an element of truth in what they say. By accepting and acknowledging this, it is easier to deal with those situations in which they might well be wrong.

3. Make it clear when you are only speculating, and when you consider them to be speculating as well

Because of their natural desire to draw or reach conclusions, there is always the danger that Js will take a general speculation on your part as a stated fact, as something to be worked upon or taken as agreed. It is not difficult to imagine the problems that arise when working with Ps! Sometimes it may be necessary to preface remarks to a J with words like, 'I'm only thinking aloud at the moment, and just thought I'd test your reaction'.

4. Ask them questions about their decision processes

Judgers have a habit of 'making pronouncements' at meetings. Everyone may be wrestling with a complex problem and the J is quite likely to come up with a phrase such as: 'It's quite obvious that there's only one thing to do here and that is . . .'. Interjections like this can be irritating! They can also catch other people off their guard and make them feel threatened (because they hadn't noticed how obvious the solution was) – at times like that it is always useful to buy some time, and so it is a good ploy to ask the J to explain his/her process of thought which brought about that particular conclusion. If the J is right, then you will all have benefitted, if s/he has just been too hasty, then her/his impetuousness is exposed.

5. Let the Judgers organize data collection and reviews

Judgers are born organizers, and preparing documents and review processes plays to their strengths and also relieves Ps from the stressful demands of getting everything together on time!

It is worth remembering that Judgers are never as certain about things as they sound, and that they tend to hear Perceivers making decisions when they haven't – so beware! It is also interesting to notice how very often Js define a problem by its solution – for example: 'the problem is, we haven't enough staff . . .' 'the problem is, we need a different telephone system . . .'.

How to keep Ps from procrastinating

If Judgers can cause problems by jumping to conclusions and being too hasty, then Perceivers cause them by being unwilling to be decisive, and always wanting to wait a little longer in case something will turn up and throw new light on the problem or give new opportunities or expand our range of choices.

1. Give them plans in advance so that they can spend time alone thinking about them

Perceivers put their energy into collecting data when they are extraverting, and they put their energy into sifting and organising data when they are introverting, and so they are more likely to be able to cope with your plans if they can reflect upon them alone, in their introvert mode, rather than if you confront them with them in person, for an immediate response. Note that with Js it was a question of giving them any *new* information in advance.

2. Acknowledge the worthwhile new information beneath the annoying style

Despite the fact that Ps can be infuriating in bringing in new information just as a decision is about to be made, it is important to note that very often their observations may be pertinent and important.

3. Make it clear when you have made a decision, have set a deadline or are about to act, and when you want them to do the same

This is one of the most difficult areas between Js and Ps, and it is important that great care is taken to ensure that both sides understand what has been said and heard. Ps have an inbuilt ability to misrepresent or misunderstand deadlines, and just as Js can think that decisions have been taken when they haven't, so Ps can think that decisions have not been taken when they have.

4. Ask questions which make them think about the order and direction of their thoughts

Perceivers are in the business of amassing information (through their senses and intuition), so carefully designed questions can help them to organize this information rather than move off into new spheres of questioning and collecting yet more information. 'Do you think we might have a series of training days on publicity?' is much more likely to get a positive response than 'What on earth can we do about publicity?'. In group discussions or team meetings Ps may well appear to be less certain than Js, and it may be that their rather more hesitant viewpoint needs to be coaxed out of them.

5. Arrange frequent feedback sessions

When delegating work to a Perceiver, it is often helpful to arrange feedback sessions during the course of the work, rather than leave it until the deadline arrives. Ps tend to take on more than they can cope with, they are not selective. For them, the process of selection comes *during* the work rather than before it. Also, as the work progresses, Ps may well have further ideas about how it might be done, or improved (especially if they are also iNtuitives), and so built-in feed-back sessions can help the Ps along but also may develop and improve the overall task.

How to keep Ts from trampling all over people's feelings

Thinkers seem to have an inbuilt tendency to cause hurt when they don't mean to, and when this happens they are very often completely unaware of the fact. A Feeler team-member can feel very hurt because a T has not come back to them with some information, and s/he may brood over this omission and work out a whole host of reasons why the T has acted in this way. The T may have completely forgotten about it, or decided that the information was so trivial that there was no need to get back to the F. A simple decision, or oversight by the T, may have kept the F awake for several nights! We have to discover ways of relating to Thinkers in order to prevent them trampling over people's feelings.

1. Don't respond when your feelings are strong

When you are hurt by a T, write down just what it was that upset you. The next day, or at a convenient time when the immediate feeling of hurt has passed, tackle the T with the problem. Don't do this when you're still in a highly charged emotional state as Ts need to respond to the logic of a complaint – they cannot cope with emotions in a logical way.

2. Make it clear what it was that caused the hurt or anger

Write the points down as clearly as possible, and then ask the T why s/he acted in this particular way. Was s/he aware of the fact that what was said or done was hurtful, and that it could have been expressed in a much better way if s/he had done or said x, y or z? Ts are usually ready to listen to complaints, and they are prepared to change their style if they can see that this is a logical thing to do. What they are not prepared to respond to, or what they find particularly difficult to handle, are emotional outbursts, or anything which seems to them to be illogical or manipulative.

3. Listen to their side and let them know that they are understood

Thinkers usually have a reason for saying the things that they say, or for acting in a particular manner. Try to find out what it is that they are trying to communicate, and let them know that their position and reasons are understood. Only then should it be suggested that there might be better ways of achieving what they want to achieve – and Ts will listen to what you have to say when they realise that you understand them and that you have ideas which might make them more effective.

4. Explain feelings in objective terms and show the logic in them

If Thinkers are to understand how feelings have been hurt, they need to have this explained to them as coolly and as objectively as possible. They are looking for logical sequences and meanings and if you can show them that their behaviour has been misunderstood, misinterpreted, or based on poor reasoning, then they are more than likely to be prepared to stop and listen to what you have to say. As one Thinker put it, 'I respect someone who can tell me in a calm way that I hurt his/her feelings, who will let me explain why I said something, and then show me that there is a different way to say it. I learn from being challenged like that'.

5. Suggest alternative ways of expressing themselves

Don't just complain, try to find a positive alternative line of action that could have been pursued. This can then help a Thinker in future situations.

How to keep Fs from failing to deal with the 'tough stuff'

Feeling types are notoriously weak when it comes to either receiving or giving criticism. They don't like it directed towards themselves, and when looking at other people, much prefer to focus upon what is right or good about them rather than on what they are doing wrong. In team situations Fs may hold back from giving critical comment, and they may manipulate others to ensure they are not hurt themselves.

1. Don't give feedback when you are feeling very critical

When you need to be very critical of an F, wait until you are ready to handle it. It may delay things for a while, but can save a lot of time in the long run!

2. Prepare by listing all the things they did well

Because Fs think you are criticizing them as people when you are critical of something that they did or said, it is important that, before making critical comment, you establish a common ground of well-being, so that critical comments are more likely to be received within the context of general approval.

3. 'And,' rather than 'but'

Instead of saying: 'You did this well *but* you didn't do that well', try to phrase your words more like: 'You did this well *and* I think you will find improvements can be made on that by . . .'.

4. Be co-operative and helpful

Feelers are more likely to respond if they think that you are with them, rather than 'over-against' them. In a team situation it is therefore important to emphasize the corporate nature of the enterprise. Problems faced are *our* problems rather than *yours*, and we need to work out how *we* are going to respond rather than ask them how *you* are going to deal with the matter.

5. Point out the impersonal factors at work

Feelers tend to see and interpret things personally; they are always involved in a situation themselves, and are inclined to take personal pride in success and personal responsibility for failure. They very often need help in finding an impersonal frame of reference, help in stepping out of the situation and seeing it more objectively. For example, someone being made redundant may be the victim of high interest rates rather than of poor workmanship, and s/he may need help to internalize an awareness of the reality of impersonal forces.

All the above points are concerned with relating to Feelers, and helping them to accept criticism, or take on board the hard decisions that often have to be taken by organizations and other people. Feelers often give the impression that they need to be protected, with the result that people may not say what needs to be said for fear of hurting them. What we need to discover are ways of enabling Fs to deal with the 'hard stuff' rather than continuing to protect them from facing up to it.

This also applies to Fs who have the responsibility for being critical, or for taking the hard decisions which affect other people. Susan Brock, a psychologist and organizational consultant in Minneapolis, describes three processes which F managers often seem to go through: 'First, they deny that there is a problem, then they say "We're working on it", which really means that they are trying to be understanding and giving them the benefit of the doubt but not giving any clear negative feedback. Third, they decide that they've had it and go in and take the person's head clean off!'

Feelers in this position need to go through the list that has been explained above, and adapt it to their own position. Just as a Thinker needs to be aware of his/her tendency to move in too quickly, so a Feeler needs to be aware of his/her tendency to avoid moving in at all, or moving in too slowly. After that, the same pattern applies: find positive things to say, be co-operative and point out the impersonal forces at work.

How to keep Ss from getting stuck on specifics

Sensers and iNtuitive types can work together on committees or in teams for many years, and still find that they fail to communicate; the one seeing the other as being too airy-fairy, and, in return, being seen as stuck-in-the-mud and incapable of responding positively to change. This section is written for all those iNtuitives who have difficulty in communicating with Sensers!

1. Think of a fundamental reason for this change

If you have an idea for a change, what is the fundamental, over-riding, all-important reason for this change? How will it save money? Ease negotiation? Help people? Solve the problem? If you want to get a Senser involved with an idea, then it must be presented to him/her in a way that can gain their interest – and that means that it must be practical, relevant, and understandable. It has been said that Ss have a rule: 'If it isn't broken, don't mend it', which means that they are not interested in improvement for the sake of improvement, but only in improvement if it solves a problem, releases resources for other things, and enables their prime objective to be reached more easily, more quickly, or more cheaply.

2. Remember the sensory origins of the idea

What made you think of the idea in the first place? Where were you? What prompted the thought? What was the problem? Sensers take in information through their senses, and so if you want them to share in your enthusiasm, then you must share with them the sensory perception which stimulated your thinking. If you are able to do this, it might communicate itself to them as well. For example: 'For the third time this week I found the door locked, and thought that there must be a way of ensuring access to the building . . .'.

3. Find a short and memorable way to communicate

INtuitives can be wordy (especially if they are also Ps), and words can be qualifying; and far from making things more precise they can, at times, be bewildering. Sensers prefer to keep things short and snappy. The long explanations can come after they have expressed their interest and given a commitment!

4. Give them an action plan

Sensers like a logical sequence, they like to begin at the beginning and work through to the end. It is always a help to show them where an idea fits into a plan. INtuitives sometimes get so interested in their particular idea that they give insufficient attention to what comes before and after it. If you are trying to persuade an S to move, then it helps your cause considerably if you can show where it all fits together. Do not, however, make the action plan itself too specific, or you face the danger of them getting hooked onto something that is not integral to your idea, and missing out on your main purpose.

5. See if there is something similar already in existence

If some other organization has changed to this system, if someone else has held their meetings at that conference centre, if some other church has managed a stewardship campaign . . . then, the Ss on your group might be willing to consider it. They tend to like to see something that already exists, and then improve on it, rather than branch out into the unknown. INtuitives sometimes find this a difficult thing to do, as they like to grapple with the unknown and are sometimes less interested if they know that someone else, somewhere else, has come up with a similar idea!

6. Ask Senser friends to test out your ideas first

It is a good idea to prepare your ground well before presenting Ss with a new idea; they will naturally be looking for the pitfalls. Even when you think you have done the necessary work, see if you can arrange for other Ss to listen to your case, or read through your papers first. It takes an S to spot the specifics which may scupper your plans.

How to keep Ns from never leaving never-never land

INtuitives can be fascinating people to work with – if you are an iNtuitive as well; if you are a Senser they can be infuriating! INtuitives can be so concerned with the 'big picture' and with what is going to happen, that they can appear to have no understanding of detail, and little sense of its importance. If you are an S working with Ns, then here are a few suggestions to lighten your load.

1. Let them talk about their vision, before you give them your details

INtuitives need time to explore ideas, so let them have it. Let them pursue their ideas while you work out in your own mind where and how the details fit together. When you are satisfied that you have a grasp of the details that need to be considered, then go back to the Ns and show how these details underpin their vision – or, how that vision cannot be substantiated by the facts that are known. But first, listen to their vision, then they are more likely to listen to your views.

2. Set the details in the context of when they were a new and exciting idea

INtuitives are more likely to stop and consider details if they are given as being part of an important 'big plan'. Thus detailed questioning about specific shopping habits may begin to appeal if they are seen as being part of the background to seeing if a large, unsightly piece of local waste-land might be transformed into a new shopping complex. Within church services, certain parts of the ritual might be exceedingly irritating or boring to iNtuitives, but if they fasten onto the idea that this is a piece of ritual that unites worshippers all over the world, and in fact has been a part of the liturgy of persecuted people, bringing them hope and vision in their struggle against totalitarian and racist regimes, then there is a good chance that the specific details will take on a new significance for them.

3. Give them the framework before the details

INtuitives see the world in broad sweeps, in overall patterns, within a framework of possibilities. Details only really make sense to them as parts of the greater whole. If you want them to focus upon details, ensure that you present those details within the context of the general framework and not in isolation.

4. Don't judge progress by tangible results, but by the development of concepts

Thinking time is important to an N. S/he may take what appears to be an inordinate amount of time getting started on a project and producing tangible results, but s/he may well have been working away on it in his/her mind, re-arranging ideas, exploring new avenues of thought and reflecting on all the options before settling down and appearing to 'start'. I know an iNtuitive who spends at least the first 30 per cent of the time in any exam reading all the questions and reflecting on which he is going to answer. Only then does he pick up his pen and start writing, by that time virtually all of the people around him are well into their answers.

5. To get them grounded, throw them a line, don't shoot them down

It is important that Ns dream dreams – that is how progress comes about, but the time comes when their dreams have to be grounded and the practical details worked out. That is where they need the help of Sensers. Sensers can either try to deflate Ns by rubbishing their ideas and pouring scorn and ridicule on their impracticability, or they can encourage them by making specific suggestions which allow their ideas to become more earthed and more open to critical comment.

How to keep Es from externalizing everything

Extraverts enjoy talking things through with other people, but they can fall into the trap of talking everything through with everyone, to such an extent that colleagues can become infuriated. Extraverts, in externalizing things, and getting their energy from the external world, can reach the stage of merely reflecting other people's views rather than expressing their own.

1. Ask them to ask themselves a few more questions

Encourage them to stop and work out what *they* think before asking everyone else for their opinion.

2. In meetings encourage them to listen rather than speak for a time

Extraverts tend to do their thinking while they are speaking, and so they are more interested in talking than in listening. When discussing new ideas or planning, there will be a tendency for the Extraverts to hog the floor, and be more interested in the development of their own thinking than in the ideas of other people. They may need to be told that it is now time for them to stop and listen to others, especially to the Introverts.

3. In meetings, build in time for interaction

Extraverts can become restless if there are insufficient opportunities for them to relate to others. In meetings, things will flow much better if there are built-in opportunities for them to stop and chat things over.

How to keep Is from isolating themselves

Introverts are quite content to fade into the background. When working with teams it is essential that their contributions are not overlooked. The advice for dealing with Is is almost the mirror image of that for dealing with Es.

1. Ask them to ask others a few more questions

Introverts tend to mull things over and then come out with their conclusions. They need to be encouraged to discuss things with other people *before* they make their mind up.

2. In meetings encourage them to speak rather than listen for a time

Great collusion can take place between Es and Is. The Extraverts like to talk and the Introverts like to listen; the roles must be reversed for at least part of the meeting if each is to make the contribution that s/he is capable of making.

3. In meetings, build in time for reflection

Introverts like to have time to think, and are not happy with more and more information being given to them without the time and opportunity for reflection. Just as Extraverts need time to talk it through, so Introverts need time to think it through.

If we are to work together effectively, then it is essential that we understand each other, what makes us 'come alive' and what are the things that we will do anything at all to avoid facing up to. Each of us comes to a group with specific type preferences, and the functioning of the group will be far less stressful if those preferences are recognized and worked on.

Using type to approach problems

It is possible to use the four inner processes (Sensing, iNtuition, Thinking and Feeling) to focus upon specific problems, and to identify and list what each 'function' has to offer. We need to take note of the fact that we all find it easier to deal with some of these than with others – because those four processes are our dominant, auxiliary, third and fourth preferences. It is therefore a useful exercise to begin on an individual basis, and then to share insight on a group or team basis.

Imagine that some major problem has to be faced and resolved. You can then use your knowledge of type to raise specific questions, and in so doing, assure yourself that you are looking at the problem from different aspects, including those which do not come easily to you. Mention is made of this process in the very useful booklet by Hirsh and Kummerow *Introduction to Type in Organizations*[2]. For example:

Questions raised by Sensing
- What do we actually *know*? What are the facts of the matter?
- What are people doing about it at the present moment?
- What is the time-scale? What are the parameters within which we are having to work?
- Is there any other relevant information which ought to be considered?

Questions raised by iNtuition
- What are the possibilities?

- Are there any other ways of looking at the problem?
- Are there any other problem-solving routes that could be taken?
- What do the facts actually *mean*?
- Are there any other similar problems that we could refer to, and see how they were resolved?

Questions raised by Feeling
- How important is it to me/us that a solution is found in one way rather than another?
- What values are implied by the various possible solutions?
- How will the possible outcome affect the people involved?
- Is there a commitment (by whom?) to implement a solution?
- What effect is the eventual outcome likely to have upon group/team relationships?

Questions raised by Thinking
- What are the arguments for and against each possibility?
- What are the likely consequences should the possibilities be implemented?
- What costs are involved?
- What are the potential benefits and disadvantages of each possibility?
- What would happen if no action were taken?
- What else is likely to happen in other areas that might have a bearing upon this problem?

We use our Perception function in this exercise by ensuring that we are open and questioning in our approach; we use our Judgement in determining some form of timetable which allows us to give each process a reasonable amount of time and enables us to move on to the next one; we use our Introversion to reflect on what each process illuminates; and we use our Extraversion when discussing the ideas with other members of the team.

Type character and organizations

William Bridges is head of an American firm which specializes in helping organizations deal with change and transition, and he has recently been working on ways of discovering the type or character of organizations. He says:

I recognized very early that organizations differed in how they dealt with change. Some companies saw change coming, and others always seemed to be caught unprepared. Some organizations took changes in stride, while others were undone by even minor ones. Some organizations were sensitive to what change did to their people; others simply announced changes and fired those who couldn't adjust.[3]

Building on the same Jungian concepts as Myers and Briggs, Bridges has worked out an 'Organizational Character Index', and has been applying this to many of the firms and companies that he is involved with. He admits that this work is still in its early stages, and does not yet have sufficient research data for it to be generally accepted and used as a tried and tested instrument, but much of what he writes makes good sense, and surely will be developed in time.

Teams can use ideas such as Bridges' with benefit, and begin to explore corporate dynamics by assessing the predominant type and style of working relationships. The ability to do this might well afford insight into how and why some people seem to 'fit' an organization better than others, and why some people experience considerable stress when working within certain organizational cultures. Using the framework which MBTI provides for individuals, one can begin to make some provisional judgements about organizations. Certainly, there is a context within which we can begin to formulate meaningful questions about organizations, groups and institutions.

Conclusion

It has been our experience that the MBTI can be of considerable help and value when applied to teams and groups in their various work situations. It can help individuals to understand themselves and to appreciate how they differ from others; it can be used to show how we can each benefit from the differing gifts that we bring to any group or team. It can be used to help team members communicate with each other more effectively; it can provide a framework for joint problem-solving; it may well shed light on the causes of interpersonal conflict; and it can be used to appreciate and respond to differing management styles more effectively.

8 Learning and Teaching Together

In her book *Gifts Differing*, Isabel Briggs Myers has this to say about the practical implications of type, particularly with respect to learning styles:

> However a subject is taught, students tend to remember only the parts that capture their attention and interest. Theoretical presentations and assignments are likely to bore the sensing students. The practical side without the theory tends to bore the intuitives. A fifty-fifty mixture can be expected to bore everybody half of the time. If students are allowed to spend most of their time on the aspects they will remember and find useful in their lives, there will be much more enthusiasm for education among its intended beneficiaries, and much more learning will take place.[1]

When considering teaching and learning in relation to personality type we need to bring together two distinct but interrelated understandings: first is to understand the type of the teacher (and therefore appreciate those things which s/he will prefer to focus on – and those aspects which s/he will have least preference for); second is to understand the type of the pupil or student, and thus to appreciate what will appear most attractive to him or her, and what might pose difficulties.

This chapter will deal with these two aspects of learning and teaching. [For those who want to explore the subject further there is a useful chapter in Keirsey and Bates' book *Please Understand Me*[2] and a very useful booklet by Meisgeier, Murphy and Meisgeier *A Teacher's Guide to Type*[3].]

Teachers and type

By understanding our own type we can gain insight into how we are likely to approach material in a teaching situation, and how we might react with students. Some of the details contained in

Chapter 7 on 'People Living Together' will be useful here, in reminding us how different preference types respond to similar or differing types. For example: a teacher who is, say, an ENTP may find students who are ISFJ particularly difficult, and it is helpful to recognize that the reason why this is so is because the students' reported preferences are the exact opposite of the teacher's. Knowing this can be of considerable help in working out how to overcome problems. Similarly, we can also begin to appreciate why a Senser teacher will probably enjoy facts more than theories, whereas an iNtuitive would probably enjoy theories more than facts. An Extravert teacher may enjoy and encourage cut and thrust discussion; a more Introverted one will probably prefer a quieter and more reflective approach.

What enthuses us, energizes us and makes us particularly interested in our subject will spill over into our teaching, thus we need to pay particular attention to how we handle material which does not inspire or enthuse us – which may be the very thing that a particular student is needing – as our handling of it can affect how students receive material and learn.

Obviously, teachers cannot be 'all things to all people', and inevitably their personality can illuminate (or destroy) the subject matter being handled. But by being sensitive to those areas which we find difficult or less attractive, we can ensure that good communication takes place – even when we are dealing with our 'less preferred' functions and are involved with students who have different, even opposite, type formulae.

Students and type

A child's dominant function is thought to develop from about the age of six – but it may be as late as fourteen. The auxiliary function develops later, towards the end of adolescence. It is thought that if the auxiliary is less well developed, then the child will have greater difficulty in adapting to differing teaching styles. Because it is not practicable to give children a Myers Briggs questionnaire, special work has been done to devise a way of assessing children's type. This is known as the 'Murphy–Meisgeier Type Indicator for Children' (MMTIC).

This chapter will not deal with the specific details of children's work, but rather will focus on how different personality types approach learning situations. Much of the material here will be familiar from earlier chapters, but it demonstrates how our understanding of type can be of value in differing situations.

Extravert students	Introvert students
Like variety and action in the classroom	Like working on their own
Talk to others about their ideas	Can become engrossed and absorbed by their ideas
Show energy and enthusaism	Very often conceal their interest
Express thoughts and feelings openly	Let others speak first
Are often friendly and talkative	Often fade into the background
Can be distracted easily	Don't like interruptions
Enjoy 'cut and thrust'	May not like spontaneous questions
Work out their thinking whilst talking	Like to think about an idea before talking about it

Sensing students	iNtuitive students
Like precise instructions	Like the chance to be original
Focus on the present	Focus on the future
Prefer skills already learned	Prefer learning new skills
Work steadily and patiently	Work in fits and bursts of inspiration
Prefer facts and measurable things	Prefer ideas and possibilities
Like things presented sequentially	Appear to be less concerned with order and sequence

Enjoy detail	Dislike taking time for precision and often get facts wrong
Like tradition	Want variety and spontaneity
Solve problems by using tried and tested methods	Enjoy designing new methods to solve problems

Thinking students	Feeling students
Prefer personal achievement to group work	Prefer sharing information with others in groups
Enjoy debates and disagreements	Want harmony and avoid confrontation
May enjoy talking with teachers more than with other students	Generate 'class warmth' and are sensitive to everyone's feelings
Need to succeed	Need to be praised
Are analytical and look for flaws	Enjoy subjects which have a human dimension
Need to have information presented clearly	Need to be able to relate to the teacher
Want to know *why* things are done as they are	Look for the good in people and in events
Are interested in grades and marks	Have difficulty in accepting criticism

Judging students	Perceiving students
Like to get things settled and sorted out	May start a new piece of work before finishing the first
Do not like unfinished work	Like to move around and not be tied to a desk

Don't like surprises	Are curious and like surprises
Like to work to set timetables and schedules	Like to be carried along by a subject
Invariably hand their work in on time	Are often late finishing their work
Work best when it is planned and prepared carefully	Cope well with the unexpected and unplanned
Tend to be in control of their work	Often feel that their work controls them
Usually have good study habits	Are often unorganized, with too many things left to the last moment
Like to make decisions	Often see their work as play

Teaching by type

Teachers need to remember that it is often easier to teach Extraverts, as they are more likely to show interest in the subject by their facial expressions and by their willingness to take part in discussions and to ask questions. Introverts, equally, may be extremely interested but they will tend to keep that to themselves, and it may not be until you receive written work back from them that you realize that their interest had been aroused. Extraverts enjoy the chance for a break and to talk things over, and it is good to build discussion-time into any lesson. Introverts, on the other hand, will appreciate some time of quiet to reflect on the subject and sort out the ideas in their head. Although Extraverts like the chance to talk things over, they are also more easily distracted, and classes can be disrupted by them rather more easily.

iNtuitives

INtuitives love the chance to approach their study-subjects on a wide canvas. They like things to be open-ended, with questions being raised and with the chance to explore ideas and possibilities. For them, learning can be a great joy if the teacher is able to capture their imagination and find ways of allowing them to engage with the subject and explore side issues and all manner of related ideas. They prefer open-ended work and can get bored with a great deal of specific detail. When work needs to be done that demands close attention, iNtuitives are likely to make mistakes, and can very soon lose interest.

Sensers

Sensers like study subjects to be practical and logical. They tend to be good with their hands and may well prefer practical work to theoretical discussion. They also tend to like an orderly approach to the material in hand, and will probably respond with enthusiasm to video or audio cassettes, films and field-work. Sensers are often good at detailed work, especially if they can see how it fits into some end-pattern. When setting work for Sensers, make it quite clear what is expected and try not to leave too many things 'in the air'.

Feelers

Feelers like to build up a relationship with their teacher. Plenty of smiles and an interest in them as people (their likes and dislikes, their friends and hobbies) will bring rich rewards in terms of commitment to the subject. Feelers need encouragement, and teachers should be lavish in their praise and appreciation. When work is not up to standard, Feelers need careful feedback. They want to do well, they want to please you, and so less-than-adequate work is a problem for them as they don't want to upset you and they don't want to do anything to destroy the atmosphere of trust and mutual recognition. Teachers need to remember that Feelers put *themselves* into their work, and so criticisms about work are often interpreted personally – as criticisms of themselves as people. Feelers tend to like subjects and material that are people-centred, or that tend to be concerned with harmony; they are less drawn to technical abstractions, and prefer not to be engaged in cut-and-thrust argument. Group work and joint endeavours are usually very acceptable, and they are also conscious of other members of the class and like to feel that they too are drawn into things.

Thinkers

Thinkers are much more concerned with getting to know their

subject than with getting to know their teacher. What is important to them is that the material is presented well, in a logical and orderly manner, and that it all makes sense. Thinkers are not wanting to be involved in a relationship unless it is one of respect in which they can value the teachers for their competence and knowledge of the subject. They prefer objective situations and enjoy problem-solving; they are less inclined to be captivated by human-drama situations in which emotions seem to be as important as logic. Like the Sensers, Thinkers like to be given clear and concise instructions. Teachers need to be sensitive to the way in which they give feedback to Ts, for they can be devastated by failure, and it is important that the teacher is able to give reasons for their marks and suggestions as to how the subject can be tackled more effectively in the future.

Perceivers

When teaching Perceivers, remember that they have a tendency to take on more and more things and to fail to meet deadlines. They will invariably have problems getting work in on time, and you will need to be sensitive to the problems that they may well get into over this. Working through the night to meet a deadline is not unusual for a P student, and they may have crises which need to be resolved in having too many pieces of work outstanding and not knowing how to sort them out and plan a response. Perceivers have problems in recognizing when decisions have been taken, and teachers need to be clear in their instructions, and then to check that they have actually been understood! It is often worthwhile to have an 'interim look' at a P's work, as there is always the likelihood that s/he hasn't even begun on it yet – or that, having begun on it, s/he has been distracted into following something else up. Perceivers can be good students to have around, they enjoy new ideas and following up secondary issues; they like a subject to develop, and they tend to be interested in exploring different aspects of what they are studying. Their open-ended approach often means that they fail to draw conclusions, and when they do reach a conclusion, they are always likely to change it when they have thought of another point!

Judgers

Judging students like to know where they stand, they like to be able to depend upon the teaching method, the person who is teaching, and the times when the lessons begin and end. A change of venue, a change of teacher, or a sudden change of direction in a lesson is more difficult for them to cope with. They can experience flexibility as being oppressive. Lessons for Judgers need to have a shape, and items under discussion need to be finished rather than be left in the air and finished the next lesson. Judgers have a tendency to jump to conclusions, and are more interested in straight-lines than in circumnavigation! Within a classroom situation they can be relied upon to help, and are good at getting things and people organized; they make ideal monitors. Lessons running over time can be a problem for Js: they like to have a 'contract' with the teacher and they expect it to be honoured. Running a recent Myers Briggs Workshop, a J tutor became quite flustered when an opening session ran half an hour over the allotted time; all the participants were fascinated with the material and wanted to know more and discuss things, but the tutor was so aware of the fact that he had promised to finish by 9.45p.m. that the last quarter of an hour was really painful for him – but not for the workshop!

An understanding of type can be of real assistance to a teacher, and can help to explain the variety of responses that a single lesson can elicit. Sensitivity to the students can therefore mean extra work for the teacher who will want to adapt his or her material and teaching style to different times and places. But the satisfaction to be gained by knowing that real learning is taking place is well worth the extra effort.

Part Three

9 Looking at the Church

Whatever else the Church may be, it is most definitely a social organization. It can be observed, charted, studied, and measured in a variety of ways. Its patterns of leadership may be compared with patterns of leadership in other organizations; its conditions for entry, its internal communications systems and its understanding of itself are all observable phenomena. We can study its divisions, its teachings, its finances and its work. We can also study its membership, and the MBTI is a helpful tool in this process.

By looking at the type profile of members of a congregation, for instance, we can draw a number of conclusions about the style and content of that church's life and teaching. By looking at the type profile of people who are selected for the Ministry, we can draw further conclusions, and we can also look at the type profile of different kinds of sector ministers, or bishops or church administrators. We can see if there are any questions to be asked, any light to be shed on the activities of the churches, any suggestions that might be made. We have seen already, towards the end of Chapter 7 that work is now being done to see if we can formulate type profiles of organizations, in much the same way that we can study type in relation to individual people. This chapter is concerned with looking at type in relation to the institution of the Church.

Church membership

We still have little data to work on at the moment, so the conclusions drawn in the next few pages are extremely tentative and certainly not statistically accurate or reliable. However, we do feel that a pattern is emerging and that we can begin to suggest certain traits, and provide one or two hypotheses which can be thought over and verified or disproved over time. Thus, for instance, it would seem that mainline Anglican Churches in Britain have a special attraction for Introverted Feeling and Judging types (IFJs); that it is extraordinarily difficult for these churches to attract Sensing – Perceptive types (SPs) into membership, and that Thinking types find membership less congenial than Feeling types. Whilst most of our own work has been done within the Anglican tradition, we suspect that other mainstream churches in Britain may not be too dissimilar.

The Tables that follow (*which must be interpreted with extreme caution*) show some interesting findings relating to the percentage of different Personality Types found in a number of different samples.

Table 1 Distribution of indicated preferences (percentage).

Sample	*E or I*		*S or N*		*T or F*		*J or P*	
US population	75	25	76	24	50	50	55	45
Curates (British province)	29	71	52	48	40	60	55	45
English diocese (POT)	38	62	26	74	36	66	70	30
English diocese (POT)	33	67	33	67	44	56	72	28
English diocese (clergy)	31	69	28	72	28	72	66	34
English diocese (laity)	29	71	53	47	6	94	58	42
English diocese (laity)	20	80	65	35	30	70	80	20
English diocese (laity)	22	78	44	56	33	67	66	34
Theological college	31	69	43	57	35	65	66	34
Theological college	33	67	46	54	40	60	86	14
US clergy	61	39	43	57	32	68	70	30

POT = Post Ordination Training – i.e. men and women in their first three years in the ordained ministry.

Table 2: Distribution according to temperament (percentage)

	SJ	SP	NT	NF
Theological college students	36	7	16	41
English diocese (laity)	32	2	18	48

Table 3 Distribution according to type in a theological college (percentage)

ISTJ	ISFJ	INFJ	INTJ
14	10	14	10
ISTP	ISFP	INFP	INTP
2	6	8	6
ESTP	ESFP	ENFP	ENTP
—	—	12	—
ESTJ	ESFJ	ENFJ	ENTJ
2	10	6	—

What tentative inferences can be drawn from the above Tables? It is important to emphasize that, because of the smallness of the samples we can only at this stage gain some *general impressions*; more detailed and sustained work needs to be carried out before we can draw any reasonably reliable conclusions. Nevertheless:

- Although the majority of the population are Extravert (NB: We do not have figures for the UK, so must use those for the USA), Introverts seem to be attracted to church membership in greater proportion to their overall numbers (and Extraverts, conversely, less so). Church-going would appear to be an Introvert activity.
- American clergy would appear to be more Extravert than British clergy.
- It is difficult to discern any clear pattern between Sensing and iNtuition with the figures that we have. However, given the likelihood that there are significantly more Sensers within the population at large, then it appears that the church attracts a greater proportion of the available iNtuitives than it does the available Sensers.
- Although it would seem that Thinkers and Feelers are evenly distributed within the population, in every sample that we have taken in church-related workshops, the Feeling types out-number the Thinking types very significantly, suggesting that church culture is definitely F.
- It seems likely that laity are more F than the clergy. Given also that most clergy are F rather than T, it means that T clergy might have more difficulties within parochial ministry, where they work within a structure which makes greater demands upon their less preferred function. There seems to be evidence to suggest that Thinkers find it more difficult to settle within churches, and clergy who are Thinking types seem to gravitate into sector ministries where they would appear to outnumber Feelers.
- The church appears to attract slightly more Judgers than Perceivers than their distribution within the general population would warrant. Our figures are too small, and insufficient work has been done to draw any real conclusions.
- When we look at temperament, there are significant differences between the four, and it appears that the NF culture of the churches does indeed dominate the others, followed by the SJ

temperament. NTs are significantly fewer, and the Table on temperament shows just how small the involvement of SPs is.

What we appear to have therefore, are churches primarily made up of Introverts (operating in an Extravert culture), with a tendency towards iNtuition (within a climate which is largely made up of Sensers) with a high proportion of Feelers (with Thinkers under-represented), and with perhaps a slight bias towards a preference for Judging. This is a brief type profile. A temperament profile shows that there is a very strong bias towards NFs and also that the churches have little contact with the SPs, and also that NTs are under-represented.

These are overall pictures. We need further information on how these impressions might be broken down for different congregations. We also need to examine whether different patterns of churchmanship, differing attitudes towards scripture and theological traditions, different social classes and geographical locations have any significant bearing upon these trends, and what influence, if any, the charismatic movement has.

The implications of type for worship and evangelism

Once we have ascertained the type profile of a congregation – or at least become aware of its possible make-up – then we can begin to ask questions about how we communicate with the different types, and what style of worship, what form of preaching, what mix of hymns and music are most likely to feed and nourish rather than alienate.

With many churches emphasizing the unity of the Body of Christ centred on the Eucharist, and with the growing experience and challenge of the ecumenical movement, we need to reflect on how a single act of worship can 'speak' to different personality types. Are there inevitable gaps? Is there value in having more than one 'central act of worship' – with a deliberate emphasis on different styles and approaches, music and preaching? We know of one church which places great emphasis upon its morning Sung Eucharist, which is very F in its approach; this is the principal service of the day. But there is also a very quiet, traditional early morning service and a very formal choral Mattins and Evensong. In recent months it has begun a Taizé-style Eucharist at 8p.m., and it has been interesting to see how popular this has become and to note that very few of the congregation attend any of the earlier services. The simple, repetitive chants, the times of quietness, and the generally more reflective approach seem to be filling a need, but the 'success' of this service is at the cost of admitting that the idea of the church having one major service which is its central act of worship is no longer appropriate.

Another way forward, which already happens to some extent, is for different churches to concentrate on one particular aspect, one particular style of worship, leaving other churches to concentrate on other emphases. Although this may make sense in theory, it demands from the various congregations a measure of trust and mutual affection and understanding which is sadly rare in our experience! In any case, such differences as exist at the moment are primarily based upon doctrine and the quirks of history, and not upon an understanding of personality type!

We can do no more than raise the issue: What forms of service? What types of worship? What approaches to corporate religious experience do we need to explore and develop in order to meet people in their strengths and their preferred functions? These are all questions which each congregation need to address.

It is an interesting exercise to sit and look through the hymn book and attempt to assess which particular preference the hymns seem to be focusing on. There are a great many F-type hymns with an emphasis upon a close personal relationship with God, which satisfies our need for belonging, harmony and acceptance; examples might be 'What a friend we have in Jesus' or 'At even, 'ere the sun was set'. There are many I hymns, which focus upon the inner journey such as: 'The Lord's my Shepherd' or 'Jesu lover of my soul'. Hymns which focus upon the senses might be 'O sacred head sore wounded' or 'All things bright and beautiful', whilst those which are more iNtuitive would include 'Father, Lord of all creation' and 'Jesus shall reign where'er the sun'. T hymns might include 'Immortal, invisible, God only wise' and 'All people that on earth do dwell', whilst E hymns might include 'We have a Gospel to proclaim' and 'Shine Jesus shine'. Those who have the responsibility for choosing hymns for public worship might well benefit from checking their lists to see how biased their selections are!

An understanding of type can also be helpful when considering evangelism. In our experience, when churches embark upon some form of evangelism they invariably end up doing what they were doing already, only louder! It is very often as though they were programmed in their understanding and their responses, and the energy which they put into evangelism merely reinforces what is already present. This is not to be over-critical, because there is much to be said for looking again at what we already do and discovering ways of improving it, but this sort of evangelism rarely breaks new ground. An understanding of type suggests that we should be looking at the type profile of our congregations and seeing if there are significant areas which are under-represented. We have already suggested that SP temperaments are noticeably absent from most churches, and that NTs often find the style and content of much worship difficult. No matter how hard we try to improve what we are doing, unless we break new ground and alter our style and content, we are unlikely to make much more impact upon these particular groups. We may, of course, bring in more NFs and SJs, but there still remains the problem of how to communicate Gospel insights to those who are of a different temperament.

By its very nature evangelism would appear to be an Extravert activity – although there is much more to it than church membership and church growth, and these remarks are not intended to imply that getting more people into church is its principal objective. But looking at the message which the churches proclaim through the eyes of type does suggest that both the content and the presentation need to be re-styled and re-formed according to the type preference of the hearer. A considerable amount of work has been done on demonstrating how an understanding of type can assist salespeople, and that work can also have a bearing upon the way in which Christians present their message.

INtuitive types will be excited by the possibilities of the Gospel, its cosmic scope, its worldwide fellowship transcending cultural and racial and national barriers; they will respond to Kingdom theology, to the idea of transforming the world and of being stewards of creation. Sensers will be more attracted to the specifics of the Gospel – what it actually promises, what it springs from, the written accounts and the ways in which these ideas have been made concrete by the various churches. They may be interested in the music and the architecture, and the shape and ritual of the Liturgy. They will respond to the 'here-and-nowness' of the Gospel.

Feeling types will respond to the welcome they receive, they will appreciate the care which is shown to them and the promises of the Gospel relating to wholeness, acceptance, forgiveness and healing. They will understand the image of the Church as a family, and they will respond to a Gospel which seeks to bring harmony to a broken world and support to those in pain. They will want to trust the messengers of that Gospel, and will want to build up a relationship with those who are explaining or presenting the faith. Thinkers, on the other hand, will be much less interested in building up a personal relationship and much more interested in knowing if what they are saying is true! They too, may be concerned about a broken world and people in trouble, but for them it is important that the causes are explained and a reasoned and logical response is made to the predicament that people find themselves in. To talk of love is nothing more than to talk of love, what is needed is some explanation, some rationale, some way forward which addresses the problems.

Judgers may be attracted by the values and moral imperatives contained within the Gospel, they may warm to the sense of order and authority, and see the Faith as offering them a systematic approach to life which has a well-tested and reliable response to the various crises and unexpected problems which crop up in our lives from time to time. These are the very things which would turn a Perceiver away from religion, but they can be attracted by the sense of spontaneous adventure within the Gospel, by the new insights which it can shed upon events and by the sense of there being more and more new things to discover, new experiences to reflect upon, and the sheer variety and scope of the worldwide Christian fellowship.

Each type will have its own particular preferences, and if the Gospel is to be communicated effectively, then it needs to be presented in ways which emphasize its relevance to our preferences. Without this sensitivity on the part of those who are seeking to 'spread the word', time will be spent communicating to people's least-preferred functions – which is probably a lengthy and fairly sterile process!

Church leadership and type

In this section we will look at the ways in which personality type can contribute to a greater understanding of the diversity of ministry. No one person has all the gifts needed for effective ministry, and yet everyone has something to offer. Recognizing what it is that we have to contribute, and what it is that we need from others are major steps towards understanding and experiencing what it means to be a member of the Christian Church. Ministry is shared among the people of God, but because churches are also social organizations, there is also the question of leadership. Clergy can be stimulating enablers, helping others to discover and perfect their gifts, or they can be jealous blockers, refusing to allow anything to develop unless they themselves are involved. Understanding what preferences church leaders and clergy have, and how these affect their ministry, can go a long way towards helping the congregation discover its own identity and future. The most helpful literature on this theme is again American, and in the remainder of this section we will draw heavily from it. In the introduction to their book *Personality Type and Religious Leadership* Roy Oswald and Otto Kroeger write:

> The great variety of types within any church system require differing approaches to ministry. Seminary training does not adequately prepare clergy to respond to divergent spiritual and psychological needs . . . As both of us are ordained clergy with parish experience, we see many ways the MBTI could bring insight, understanding and healing to the church. In the midst of the ambivalence and confusion of a complex role, church professionals need several good working theories. The MBTI, and the Jungian perspective from which it comes, has been an exceedingly helpful tool for clergy who learn to apply its categories.[1]

Extraverts and Introverts

Remembering that Extraverts are energized from the external world, and Introverts from within, we can see that Extravert clergy will tend to be interested in external events and energized by contact with a lot of people, and that they will tend to find overmuch reading, meditation or study tedious. Introverts, on the other hand, will be more interested in internal happenings and

LOOKING AT THE CHURCH

will find too much contact with people tiring, needing to be re-energized by reading, prayer and study. They will need time for and by themselves in order to become revitalized, whereas Extraverts will need time for relating to their family and friends.

In the parish ministry, with its constant round of meeting new people, it is a considerable advantage to be an Extravert, and Introverts can be at a disadvantage, as they can also be when cast in the role of having to lead public worship and 'enthuse people'. This can lead to a certain amount of tension or tiredness for Introverts. On the other hand, they tend to have the advantage when it comes to planning worship, leading retreats or giving spiritual direction – but they must learn to delegate people-related issues within the organization. Extraverts may have more diffi-culty in developing an interior life, and they can sometimes appear rather shallow when it comes to spirituality – 'borrowing' an introverted spirituality from the books they read. When Extraverts work well within the parish though, numbers are likely to increase and organizations flourish. When there are problems relating to people, Extraverts are more likely to visit them to get them sorted out, whereas Introverts will have a tendency to ignore them, hoping that they will go away, and under pressure, are more likely to withdraw into themselves.

Given the exposed nature of preaching, it might be expected that Extraverts will be better preachers than Introverts, but this is not necessarily the case, and Introverts can be very powerful speakers, especially if they have had sufficient time to prepare; however, they are probably not so good at spontaneous, off the cuff, repartee.

Sensers and iNtuitives

Sensers prefer dealing with specifics, with facts and realities which they perceive through their senses; iNtuitives are always looking for meaning and possibilities and relationships between variables. Many Ns move into the ministry or into church leadership as part of their search for meaning, they are looking towards the future which God is bringing about and they wish to share in the establishment of the Kingdom. They tend to look at reality holistically, and so it is not surprising that they are drawn into the ministry in a greater proportion than their numbers in the population generally. Sensers feel called into the ministry through the needs which they perceive, and they seek to serve God in practical ways.

Parish ministry is often bread-and-butter to Ss, because they see needs in a whole variety of places and can become actively involved in trying to meet them. These immediate needs can sometimes be a distraction for Ns whose minds are focused on the future; they may well be good pastors, but they are in their element when they can be thinking and planning ahead, and anticipating change. It is said that N clergy are high on innovation and low on procedure, whilst Ss are high on procedure and low on innovation. INtuitive clergy are often at their best when placed in situations which need revitalizing, where there needs to be change for the sake of survival, and where new patterns and new ideas are needed. They often need to be followed by Ss, who often have specific gifts for consolidation, organization and practical realities.

There are often striking differences in the preaching of Ss and Ns. What Ss call real, Ns may well call dull, and what Ns call imaginative Ss may call rubbish! N sermons will tend to treat scripture more figuratively, using it as a starting-off point for a wide range of possibilities, whilst Ss tend to be more literal in their interpretation of scripture, and they are more concerned to describe truth than to explore and embellish. In their preparation, Ss will want the text to 'touch' them, and they will be concerned with detail and accuracy: Ns will tend to start (perhaps) with scripture and then pull in one or two other books (or films or plays or conversations) which may (or may not) be related to the point at issue!

Sensers and iNtuitives also have a different approach to the use of symbols. To the S the cross is the cross: it is a specific and essential part of the Christian tradition relating to the sacrifice of Christ, and it engages them emotionally. To the N it can be a springboard to their imagination, bringing a vast number of meanings and interpretations: it can be a doorway into an exploration of suffering – theirs and other people's – and the sufferings of the world and creation itself. Symbols have great potential, and Ns love them.

Sermons by Ns have a tendency to be high on inspiration and low on practicality! As one person said: 'Once again we've been inspired to go nowhere'. Ss, on the other hand are high on practicality and that in itself is sufficient inspiration for other Ss but it will fail to communicate much to the Ns in the congregation.

Thinkers and Feelers

Thinking types can bring a natural scepticism to their ministry; they value the logical and analytical and look for cause and effect; they like to persuade people by logic. Feeling types prize harmony and warmth in relationships, they like to win people over by persuasion and bring human values and motives into their relationships and endeavours. In the ordained ministry Fs considerably outnumber Ts. The differences between them show up in their pastoral styles, with Ts wanting to objectify religion so that they can understand and explain it and Fs wanting to experience religion, so that they can become enfolded by it and gain value from it. Feelers can be objective and they can be good theologians, but often they get annoyed by what they consider to be the mind-games that Ts sometimes play. Thinkers, on the other hand, can be good pastors, but they don't feel the need to translate theory into meaning all of the time, and they can get impatient with what they perceive as the Fs need to be subjective about everything.

Because most clergy are F, and most female laity are also F, T males can often find themselves at a disadvantage within congregations. They want objective and logical answers to tough questions about faith and life, and most churches struggle to provide these (or simply fail to provide them, without bothering to struggle). Therefore, men, who in their daily work often hold responsible positions, tend to be subordinate in church, preferring to sink into the background and not become too involved with all the 'F activity' that surrounds them. When they are involved, it is invariably on the Finance Committee, running a stewardship campaign or having concern for the buildings and fabric. Men who are STJs tend to attend church out of a sense of duty, and men who are NTs invariably have problems with it and do not stay. However there seems to be some evidence to suggest that STJs are more likely to stick in fundamentalist churches.

The problems that T laymen have in the church, where the prevailing culture is F are perhaps even worse for T women who also have to struggle against the stereotype of all women being F! A problem which is heightened for T women when they offer themselves for ordination. It would appear that a great many T clergy find themselves in sector ministries, and, as an ENTP I reflect that out of the thirty years that I have been in the ministry only eight have been spent in the parochial ministry. The marginalization process which often takes place within the ministry for Ts is underlined even further when, as is very often the case, sector ministries come under attack from the stalwarts of the parochial system!

Something in the region of 80 per cent of the daily work of the pastor involves personal relations, and in this work, other things being equal, F-type clergy have a distinct advantage. Parishioners in distress look for clergy who will take on a loving, accepting parent role, and this fits the preference pattern of F clergy. They start from the basic premise of wanting to help people, and they see the Gospel primarily in terms of enabling people to come to a loving understanding of God and their neighbours.

In their preaching, Ts tend to produce more objective, conceptual sermons. They may be rather more like a lecture or a learned paper, but they tend to explore a central theological point. The message may offend people, or even hurt some people, but it will usually be clearly thought out. Feeling clergy tend to preach more sympathetic sermons, they are more likely to be people-orientated and strive for impact rather than logic. They want to stir people's hearts and may be more emotional than logical. At best they can communicate superbly, at worst they can manipulate unscrupulously!

Thinking clergy need Feelers to help them learn how to persuade people, acquire some of the skills of conciliation and how to arouse enthusiasm. Feeling clergy need Thinkers to help them learn how to analyse, to be less personal, to be able to act rather more firmly with people, and to keep a sense of perspective when overwhelmed by feelings of discouragement. It can be summarized thus: *Thinking clergy often need help in getting their heart in order; Feeling clergy often need help in getting their head in order!*

Judgers and Perceivers

Judgers deal with the outer world in a planned and decisive way, and they aim to control and regulate events; Perceivers deal with the outside world in a more spontaneous and flexible way: they want to understand the world and adapt to it. Clergy tend to have rather more Js than Ps in their ranks than is the case in the overall population.

Judging clergy prefer to have things planned and decided: they put their energy into organizing and work hard to ensure that their lives are regulated and orderly. They want closure on decisions, and will press for this even when they have insufficient data. On a large range of issues they will have firm and fixed opinions, even before they have considered the evidence. Perceiving clergy like to spend time taking in more information, they prefer to adapt to the world and tend to leave as many things open and as undecided as possible. Whereas something in the region of 70 per cent of male clergy are Js, the figure for female clergy is about 50 per cent – which poses the question as to whether, in a male-dominated world like the ordained ministry, it is essential for women to remain more flexible and open?

Judging clergy can bring stability and a sense of dependence to a congregation: in many ways they find the pastoral ministry easier than do Perceivers as they are more sure about ambiguous and complex issues and more precise about ethical matters. Perceivers can bring more options and ideas to a congregation, but they can often appear to be soft and indecisive. At their best they are open to new insights, masterful at handling the unexpected, and they can bring a sense of fun and spontaneity to their work. They can, however, begin too many things without ever finishing them, be indecisive when they need to be firm, and unsure of themselves when the pastoral situation calls for strong leadership. Judging clergy can be excellent leaders, firm and decisive; they can run a good organization and provide clear and constructive teaching and counselling. They do, however, run the risk of being dogmatic and dictatorial, unprepared to listen, and unwilling to deviate from the course that they have set.

In their preaching Js tend to have well-prepared and systematic material, and the congregation invariably knows where the preacher stands by the time the sermon finishes. Perceivers' sermons are often full of ideas, giving the hearer many unanswered questions and posing a wide variety of options. At the end, it may still be unclear what the preacher really wanted to get across, or what his or her views are! But when a P is preaching well, the sermon can be both fascinating and stimulating. In general terms, *J listeners have more problems with P sermons than vice versa.*

Administration

ESTJs have the reputation of being the best administrators. Their E allows for interaction and involvement with others, their S grounds them in reality and gives them an eye for detail, their T encourages them to search for rational approaches and their J motivates them to seek order, structure and make decisions. This obviously does not mean that all ESTJs are good administrators, or that you cannot be a good administrator if you are a different type, but the ESTJ configuration of preferences goes a long way to enabling a person to slot into a parish system with ease. Some people may find them too rigid, or too detached, or too concerned with detail, or not sufficiently 'other' and 'holy', but potentially an ESTJ is a good leader – whether in the field of parish administration or spiritual awareness and growth.

The opposite type is the INFP, and this type can experience real problems with administrative tasks. This does not mean that they cannot master the skills necessary, but it does mean that they need to be alert to the fact that they will almost certainly need to be especially aware of the gifts that others have to offer. Being an F they may find this relatively easy to do, but their I and their P may militate against them doing much to ensure that they enlist the support of others! It is therefore important that congregations realize the strengths of their clergy, and also the areas where they may have problems, and that they work together to ensure that there is a fullness and complementarity of ministry. The INFP will have specific gifts that ESTJs (and others) do not have, and the important thing is that we recognize the gifts of others and work to provide a context in which those gifts may flourish to the full.

Clergy pastoral work and temperament

In *Personality Type and Religious Leadership*, Oswald and Kroeger devote a chapter to exploring Keirsey and Bates' work on temperament as it impinges upon the pastoral role of clergy. They describe the four temperaments: the action-oriented pastor (SP), the intellectual, competence-seeking pastor (NT), the conserving, serving pastor (SJ) and the authenticity-seeking, relationship-oriented pastor (NF) (see pages 77 ff.).

The Sensing–Perceiving temperament

These are the hyperactive clergy, who tend to be constantly engaged in activity, where the sense of fulfilment comes from the doing rather than the achieving. Only 8 per cent of US clergy belong to this temperament – which is not surprising since few SPs are regular church members, and the clergy are enlisted from the ranks of the laity! They are down-to-earth people, practical and wanting to be in direct contact with reality, consequently they have little time for abstractions and easily become bored with the status quo and with endless meetings. They are fun-loving, spontaneous and rooted in the here-and-now.

Few SPs are prepared to undergo the rigorous academic training; they tend to be marginalized by the normal educational system anyway and see little point in subjecting themselves to a further two or three years when what they really want is 'hands on' experience. This is all to the church's loss, because when SPs do, eventually, make their way through to the ordained ministry they are often very good pastors, and the variety of the parish ministry appeals to them. Distractions, interruptions and crises are food and drink to them, and they thrive on the unexpected.

Sensing-Perceiving clergy tend to have great style! The present moment is everything, and they can respond to issues quickly and effectively. They can be entertaining and lively preachers, but are not inclined to spend much time in preparation. Their material tends to be contemporary and they shy away from the abstract and conceptual. They learn by doing and are bored by too much talk. They can make excellent negotiators because their S centres them in the present moment and their P brings spontaneity and flexibility. They often excel at children's work, and of all the different temperaments, the SPs are the most fun-loving and lively. Then often do well in Urban Priority Areas where little is predictable, where there are often many crises, and where there is a need for immediacy and a suspicion of too much theory and conceptualizing. They are likely to be found in charismatic congregations, with their emphasis upon Spirit-filled worship, liveliness and flexibility in worship.

Sensing-Perceiving clergy tend to be pragmatists, and better leaders than managers; they get bored with routine but can be highly effective in a crisis. They may neglect follow-up work, and have an inbuilt resistance to committees. They are often great individualists, and can feel constrained within traditional role-models. They do not like working to systems, standard proced-ures or hierarchical expectations.

The iNtuitive–Thinking temperament

These clergy are often visionaries who can provide strong leadership within a parish or congregation. They prize their competence and work to ensure that whatever they do is done well, they endeavour to be the best – whether it be in preaching, teaching, ordering worship or running meetings. They are often to be found working in theological colleges and seminaries, even though they are critical of them. They enjoy the pursuit of theological truth, thinking that they are not fitted for ministry until they have become competent in a whole range of skills.

Their spirituality is academically rooted, and they may want to turn their congregation into a mini theological college, and they may be saddened by the fact that many ordinary church members are not particularly interested in the niceties of theological exploration. They often move into sector ministries, and can be found at the forefront of the church's concern for justice in the world. In worship, they may be slightly more formal than other temperaments, and they will tend to be suspicious of too much enthusiasm or spontaneity.

Congregations with an NT minister find themselves pushed towards excellence, with an excitement about the future and plenty of debate and discussion about all aspects of life and work and believing. However, NT clergy may fall down somewhat on the pastoral side if this is seen as routine visiting, or talking to people for the sake of talking to people. They can, however, be good in a crisis. As one parishioner commented: 'He's very good when you are in trouble, but you've got to be in real trouble before you want to go to him!'

INtuitive–Thinking clergy have little time for sentimentality or over-personalized religion, and can feel distanced from the other temperaments because of this. They may feel isolated within church systems, and are inclined to 'work their own patch' with competence, looking at the wider church scene with a certain degree of scepticism, and sometimes with a sense of not really belonging. They can be accused of theological snobbery, and their tendency to nit-pick can be irritating. Because of an inclination to be future-orientated, NT clergy can be impatient with the church as it is, and frustrated by what they see as the innate conservatism of congregations. They love challenges, and can quickly become bored with a situation once they have come to terms with it. They are always on the look out for new problems to engage with, and prefer change to constancy (provided a rational basis for such change can be found).

They love their work and find it mentally, spiritually and physically absorbing. They have a perfectionist streak within them which others may find too demanding, and their desire for justice may push people to move too quickly. They run the risk of judging people by their intellectual competence, and may undervalue the gifts of relationship, harmony and sensitivity. They can appear to be arrogant, sometimes correctly, though not always so.

INtuitive–Thinking clergy have a high regard for competence, and they expect to find this in those who have authority; if they lose confidence in those above them they are likely to let it be known. They question virtually everything, and so are reluctant to follow orders just because they have been handed down from a higher authority. If they are seen to be critical of those in authority over them, this is as nothing compared to their self-criticism and their intense fear of being personally incompetent. They have a tendency to drive themselves too hard, and they have a need to learn how to let go and experience the gracious acceptance of God.

The Sensing–Judging temperament

These clergy are well grounded in reality and like to have structure and order around them. They are loyal members of the institution and seek to nurture others into a similar kind of commitment. Of all the temperaments, the SJs are the most dependent upon authority systems, and will support them even when they feel that they are out of touch.

Sensing–Judging clergy emphasize and focus on the fundamentals of religion, and they try to give people a simple faith and a set of ground rules which will serve them in the variety of situations in which they may find themselves. They tend to be the most traditional of clergy, and bring stability and continuity to the church. They are loyal to denominational doctrine and liturgies, and are hesitant to do anything which might appear to be outside the recognized norms – whether this be in their style of dress, the boundaries of their pastoral care, their criticisms of the institution or their patterns of belief. The only time when they are likely to challenge the authorities is when they feel that the authorities have abandoned traditional belief – thus, within the Church of England many SJs made their voices heard in the debates over the ordination of women to the priesthood, a move which many of them opposed.

The SJ temperament usually knows how to work the system, and is good at bringing about necessary change; it will usually be gradualist change, and it will not be threatening to the institution – evolution, never revolution! They are often good committee members, and are to be found at all levels of church government. NT clergy can often see what changes need to be brought about, but it takes an SJ actually to effect them!

There are a lot of 'shoulds' in the SJ's vocabulary; they have a strong sense of obligation, of loyalty to a tradition, and clear and unambiguous moral views. They know where they stand on a whole range of issues, and they teach a straightforward and understandable doctrine. They bring stability and order to congregations, are good at precision work and seldom make errors of fact. They dislike leaving things in the air and undecided, and prefer a decision to be taken even if it has to be reviewed at a later date. They usually run meetings well, and have straightforward agendas, which they keep to. They can be excellent administrators, but dealing with people is sometimes (but not always) harder for them.

These clergy are often very good generalist ministers, and can be the backbone of many societies; they can have a particular aptitude for working with the elderly or with children, and they place a great emphasis upon the importance of the nuclear family. In the United States, SJ clergy have the lowest divorce rate amongst clergy, which probably reflects their attitude towards the solemnity of vows once taken. They can be good pastoral counsellors, but like to see results and can get impatient with situations where progress is not apparent. They are something of a 'class act' and would warm to the view that if a job's worth doing then it's worth doing well. They are often involved in schemes for improving or embellishing church buildings.

The public worship of the SJs will be well designed, and will start and finish on time. It may well be quite formal, but will be done with dignity and reverence. Sermons will usually be structured and may well centre on the Word of God and remind people of the richness of their inheritance.

There is a tendency for SJs to take things literally, and they may well be rather conservative in their approach to doctrine and to scripture, and apprehensive about a more symbolic or figurative approach. They can suffer from burn-out, because of their sense of responsibility and duty. They have an awareness of all the things that they ought to be doing, and may well try and do them all themselves rather than delegate, at least that way they know that they will get done! They are good at 'grasping nettles', and prefer to get things sorted out than to allow them to hang in abeyance, and they may well have a tendency to stick to rules and regulations to the annoyance of people around them. They need to make a special effort to appreciate the work of others, for not everyone works out of a sense of duty. There are many people who work willingly and spontaneously and SJs may at times be slow to recognize this.

The iNtuitive–Feeling temperament

By far the greatest number of clergy are NF, and their proportion far exceeds the proportion of NFs in the general population. Because all NFs are engaged in some sort of search for meaning, it is perhaps not surprising that many of them follow a route which brings them into contact with organized religion, and many of them identify with the religious quest and become more and more involved with the church. They are the most idealistic of all the temperaments, and are attracted to helping roles and to an engagement with suffering. They are also the most likely of all temperaments to take on a low paid and serving occupation. They enjoy theological colleges, not as a place for theological exploration like the NTs, but as a community which will help prepare them for a lifetime of service and self-giving. They are places where they can be alongside other people and share in their journey as they invite others to share in their own.

INtuitive–Feeling clergy are the most adaptable of all (especially if they are also P) and have a willingness to take on the characteristics of whoever they are with – so they are likely to be conservative with conservatives, liberal with liberals, quiet with the quiet, and gregarious with the gregarious (even if they are also Introverts). They have gone a long way to mastering St Paul's dictum of being all things to all people. Whilst this can be a quite remarkable ability, it can also carry the danger of NFs being willing to do anything to please anyone. It can also make it difficult for them to know who they really are, as they are so prepared to change to meet the needs of a situation or to win acceptance or affection from others.

They are usually effective and good communicators, making good preachers because they believe what they are saying. This does not mean that other temperaments do not believe their own sermons, but NFs have to ensure that their own 'very being' is communicated when they preach. They can be excellent counsellors or spiritual guides, having an empathy with others, and the ability to place themselves in the other person's shoes. They may well over-stretch themselves in the service of others as they find it very difficult to say 'No' to any demand made upon them (especially if they are also P). They can be inspirational leaders and effective enablers of others. On the other hand, should their congregations not respond, they can easily become discouraged and hurt, taking it as a personal rejection.

There is a risk that they can be indecisive because they don't want to hurt anyone, and they are sometimes criticized for taking the views of the last person they talked to. They may also be rather too keen to accept the latest trend, sometimes letting their F dominate their T to an unhealthy level. Of all the four temperaments, NFs have the greatest need for being appreciated, and there is a risk that they collect around them groups of dependent people, and in that process of collusion may be doing more for themselves than for the people who are looking to them for support. They tend not to handle conflict very well, and when conflict appears they may devote their energy more to avoiding facing it than to dealing with it head on.

When other things are equal, NFs can make marvellous church leaders. They have a genuine concern for people, and will go to inordinate lengths to help and encourage others. They seek harmony and goodwill, and will bear the pain of others. They have embarked upon a spiritual journey and welcome others to join them; it is a journey that demands all that they have and all that they are, and will only end in God.

Conclusion

There must be a place within the church for all types, and it is a matter of concern that some types obviously find it more difficult to find a resting place there than others – unless we take the view that only certain types are called into membership of the Church, and that God has other areas of work, other sources of experience for those who are not called to specific church membership. This is a theological issue to be explored.

What is clear is that the Church as at present constituted appeals to some personality types more than to others. It also provides a particular culture or climate which enables some types to feel that they have a vocation within it and other types to distance themselves from it. This raises a number of questions about selection procedures, training, and the sort of ordained ministry which the churches are providing or seeking.

It is also clear that, given the variety of work to be done within the ordained ministry, no one personality type will be able to fulfil all the expectations and so, as Oswald and Kroeger say: 'We need to put a stop to the prevalent belief that clergy must be competent at everything'. They give a list of what they consider to be the typological preference for each of the most common pastoral skills (and I notice with interest that my own type does not feature in it under any category!):

Spiritual depth	INFP, INFJ, INTJ, INTP
Strong preacher	ENFJ or ENTJ
Youth ministry	ESFP or ENFP
Pastoral counsellor	INFJ, ENFP, INFP
Effective leader	ENTJ, INTJ, INFJ, ENFJ
Parish administrator	ESTJ or ISTJ[2]

$\boxed{10}$ Type and Spirituality

> For as we have many members in one body,
> and all members have not the same office:
> So we, being many, are one body . . .
> and every one members one of another.
> Having then gifts differing . . .
> Romans 12.4–8

Since Isabel Briggs Myers called her book *Gifts Differing* and prefaced it with this quotation from St Paul it is perhaps not surprising that a considerable amount of work has now been done to explore how an understanding of type can illuminate the spiritual journey. Whilst the MBTI is used a great deal in education, in human relations work, personnel and in management training, it is also used a great deal by the churches. A glance through the programmes of retreat houses in the UK, as published, for instance, in the National Retreat Association's journal *The Vision*[1], shows that a great many workshops are now being run for people who wish to explore the spiritual dimension of their life.

It has been said that 'prayer goes with the grain of our personality'. This is another way of saying that when a person has discovered what type they are, they are then more likely to find ways of praying which are appropriate to them. For just as it is possible to run your hand against the grain in a piece of wood, and discover that it is not smooth, so some people's experience of prayer and the spirituality which is offered to them in churches seems to go against their personal grain. They are left with a sense of unease, a deep feeling that it doesn't seem to come smoothly to them in the way that their observations suggest that it comes smoothly to other people. What our understanding of type makes clear is that people are different, and that they will respond to their environment and to stimuli in different ways. No one way is better or more correct than another way, they are just different. What we need to do is to learn how to appreciate the differences between people, and to recognize that these differences will also manifest themselves in the way that different people experience, understand and interpret the spiritual dimension of their lives.

So, who we are is how we pray! It sounds obvious, and yet a great many people feel considerable guilt because they are unable to find meaning, fulfilment or satisfaction in certain forms of spiritual activity, and they come to the conclusion that there is something wrong with them. There is also the parallel danger that people who have found meaning, help or inspiration in a particular form of spiritual activity then assume that this is the 'right' way ahead for all people, and embark upon a process of 'spiritual colonialism' which has the effect of marginalizing, and perhaps alienating, many of the very people they are wanting to address. We need to pray as we can, and not as we can't!

This chapter seeks to explore how type and spirituality relate to each other, and also to suggest ways in which our understanding of worship, liturgy and evangelism may be challenged and enlightened by reflecting on type. In our experience, for many churches the process of evangelism is understood as doing what they are already doing, only louder! Perhaps it would be more effective if some form of audit were to be taken of which types were already in the congregation to see if there were significant omissions, and if there were, to reflect on what this might be saying about the nature and content of the message being put across, and also about the methods of communication being used. Once again, it is our expectation that congregations will invariably find that there are noticeable types missing, as the previous chapter suggested.

Extravert and Introvert spirituality

The Introvert looks for God within; the Extravert sees God at work in the world. The one seeks to plumb new depths of awareness, stillness and silence; the other sees faith and devotion expressed in practical acts of compassion and self-giving. It is important to remember that we can all operate both as Extraverts and as Introverts, but that we *prefer* one mode to the other, and so we *prefer* one type of spirituality to the other. *Both are valid, but they are different.*

It seems very likely that most devotional books are written by Introverts, and a quick look through our bookshelves produced titles such as these, which all suggest introversion: *Journey into Christ*: *The Inner Journey*; *Encountering the Depth*; *Deeper into God*;

157

The River Within; Deep calls to God; Exploring Inner Space; A Diary of Private Prayer; Thoughts in Solitude. Introverted spirituality is very extensive in the teaching of our churches, and yet many of our church members are not Introverts – which would suggest that they might have a few problems coming to terms with the prevailing spiritual culture. At the very least they might gain the impression that introverted spirituality is the norm, and therefore the 'correct' form. This might also be one reason why we have more Introverts than Extraverts in our churches.

Introverts like time for space and quiet. They appreciate meditation and contemplation in ways which Extraverts can find quite difficult. For Introverts a Retreat is a source of refreshment, and prayer is an exercise in stillness and self-abandonment. Listening, looking, adoring . . . stillness, quiet and an openness to time . . . these are the essential ingredients of an Introvert's spirituality. Words are seldom necessary, and prayer can be just as effective when alone; indeed, the presence of other people is often an unwelcome distraction. Someone summed up their prayer before a crucifix as being an experience of: 'I look at Him, and He looks at me'.

Extraverts, on the other hand, often feel that they are unable to pray, and they feel uneasy when prayer is being discussed. They are much happier when they can become involved in some form of 'Gospel-action' and they probably need help in realizing that their thinking and action might well be a form of prayer in themselves. Retreats and Quiet Days can leave them feeling 'outsiders', and somehow 'second class' when it comes to spirituality. The fact that I took a transistor radio on my ordination retreat was not only because of a desire to keep in touch with the Test Match, but also because my thinking and praying needed the stimulus of the outside world – and yet, many years later, I still carry with me a slight sense of guilt that I was not able to free myself from worldly distractions. Or were they distractions? Might they not perhaps have been the raw material of prayer?

There is a passage in the Apocrypha in the Book of Ecclesiasticus, (Chapter 38) which, when talking about people going about their daily tasks says:

> But they will maintain the fabric of the world
> And in the handiwork of their craft is their prayer

– now that is good news to the Extravert!

In public worship, Extraverts may, in their prayers, invite people to be silent for a moment or two. That is what they mean, and the moment or two is seldom long enough for the Introvert. Conversely, when Introverts invite people to be silent, the period is likely to be experienced by Extraverts as being interminable, and their minds will be occupied with trying to work out when it will come to an end!

Because we need to be able to operate both as Extravert and Introvert, where appropriate, we need to work on recognizing what is happening when we pray. Identifying those situations which are helpful and those which are problematic may mean that we can begin to assess whether the tension emerges from the Extravert–Introvert axis. In the growth to maturity, some people find that although they are Extravert, they can become re-charged by focusing upon introvert needs; similarly, some Introverts find that being exposed to extravert activity can, at times, enrich their own inward journey.

Judging and Perceiving spirituality

A Judging attitude towards the world is one that seeks structure, order and control, whilst a Perceiving attitude towards the world prefers to remain open and flexible and is rather more passive than the Judging attitude. These contrasts reveal themselves in spirituality as well. Judgers tend to like to have things ordered, whether it be doctrine or liturgy, whereas Perceivers tend to be rather more open to many differing ideas and more spontaneous in their approach to worship.

Judgers are more likely to have a fixed idea about their devotional life, and it probably follows an orderly pattern – whether this is linked to following a specific scheme of Bible readings, regular attendance at certain services, or a particular form of prayer. They have discovered that the structure carries them through times of barrenness, and there is a sense of loyalty and commitment to the pattern that has been built up. Judgers are less likely to be influenced by the charismatic movement, and are more likely to find strength and succour in traditional forms of worship, discipline and Bible study.

Perceivers, on the other hand, may well find traditional and set ways go stale on them after a time, and they will be on the look out for new experiences and more flexible patterns. They will not dismiss the traditional, but will want to see it as available to them amidst a whole set of other options. They may well operate within a traditional context, but every now and then make 'improvements' which may irritate the Js who are affected by them; this will be to the total surprise and incomprehension of the Ps, who see nothing strange or unacceptable in their variations and modifications. The sense of being 'led by the Spirit' makes complete sense to a P, and so services may last rather longer than normal on occasion; a J will almost certainly want to be led by the Spirit in a more orderly manner! In the journey towards wholeness, Js need to work on allowing themselves more spontaneity; Ps need to come to terms with their need for discipline and orderliness.

Sensing spirituality

Sensing is a perceiving function and therefore it has to do with being open and receptive. Sensing spirituality is based in the present moment, and it has the capacity to pay attention to the here-and-now, to the environment that surrounds us, and is sensitive to external stimuli such as sound and smell, sight and touch. 'The sacrament of the present moment' sums up Sensing spirituality.

It is often simple and straightforward, and doesn't like too many abstractions and formularies. This carries an inherent danger that Ss are prone to over-simplify complex issues, and may, therefore at times have a suspicion about 'theology' – seeing it as something which obscures that which is, at heart, basically simple, being open and receptive to God.

Sensing spirituality tends to have a clear pattern, and can be very obedient (– the very word 'obedient' coming from a Latin word concerned with hearing!). Thus, there may be a clear loyalty to the Bible, or to the church, and this is accepted and doesn't need to be agonized over or subjected to a multitude of possible alternative theories or viewpoints.

Sensing prayer is simple, open and sincere: 'In God we live and move and have our being'. Sensers often like the liturgical patterns of prayer, and the Eucharist with all its symbolism, is very important to them; a late evening prayer like Compline, in a quiet chapel with one or two candles may also be especially conducive to Ss.

Posture is important to many of them, and symbols and visual aids such as candles, flowers or pictures can often help Ss in their prayers. Music can help them to relax and reflect, and a time of prayer looking at a candle with a Taizé chant in the background can be very acceptable; incense is appealing as it engages the Ss' sense of smell in their devotional life – something which an iNtuitive may find much more difficult to understand.

A weekly lunchtime series in a city centre church encouraged people to become aware of their bodies, to concentrate their minds on their breathing, and to listen to the multitude of sounds around them. Participants were then invited to take their shoes off, and in silence walk *very slowly* around the church, feeling the stones beneath their feet, listening to the sounds of silence and being aware of the colours and shape and texture of the walls and furnishings. Many of the people who came to this series found it to be of enormous help, and they returned to their work refreshed and invigorated.

Sensers like to know where they are going, and they like clear instructions. There are a high proportion of Ss in our churches, and therefore the symbols we use, the music, and the general sensual ambience is of great importance (that is one reason why people complain when it is cold!). St Mark's Gospel is said to relate to Ss because of its immediacy and direct style.

For those of us for whom Sensing is our third or least-preferred function, the question we have to ask ourselves is this: 'How do we get in touch with our senses so that the whole of our being is involved in the spiritual quest?'

iNtuitive spirituality

INtuitives perceive through their imagination; they are aware of possibilities, they are future-orientated and live in a provisional world, and their spirituality is therefore conditioned by their type preferences. They are attracted to Kingdom theology, to the idea of what God is bringing about, and they look to a future when the world will be as God wishes – a world of peace and justice, of limitless possibilities and freedom. They have a transcendent view of God, and can be captivated by allowing their minds to contemplate the splendour and the mystery and the otherness; but it is a transcendence that relates to the world and constantly challenges the world to become what it is planned to be or

161

promised to be. It is not a spirituality that seeks to escape from the world into God, but rather one that seeks to transform the world into the very likeness of God.

INtuitives are often energized by the world, for it is within the world with all its complexities and ambiguities and challenges that they meet with God, and they believe that God speaks to them in a multitude of different ways and through a vast variety of people and situations. For the iNtuitive, 'Every bush is afire with God'. They therefore tend to dislike fixed patterns and established procedures, would rather be exploring different methods, and they are always open to change. They love to dream dreams and imagine possibilities, and are willing to explore worship through music and art, through dance and drama, recognizing that for some people this will be a vehicle for the Spirit, whilst for others they must look in different places. INtuitives are more likely to be open to inter-faith dialogue, and less concerned with ensuring that 'essential truths are defended'. This does not mean that they are necessarily lax in their grasp of truth, or that they believe in 'all things for all people'; rather, they recognize that God is a God of surprises, and that He (or She) cannot be held down in the tight compartments that humankind so often wish to establish. (It will be no surprise to you to know that this paragraph was written by an ENTP!)

INtuitives often have a cosmic approach to faith, and they are fascinated by creation and its vastness and complexity. All things are possible, and they dwell upon the creative abilities of people, and like to dream about possibilities and what might be. I well remember a Dutch religious community I came across some 30 years ago whose motto was 'Live today as though tomorrow were already here', that is, if you believe that the Kingdom is about peace and justice, then live today with that commitment – a classic N approach to spirituality. INtuitive spirituality is a spirituality of hope, of realized eschatology; thus it can very easily be frustrated or marginalized by what it considers to be a narrow or too conventional and inflexible liturgy or pattern of prayer and devotion, this is especially true for Perceiving iNtuitives.

St John's Gospel speaks most clearly to the iNtuitive, with its symbolism and mysterious possibilities; as does the Book of Revelation with its promise to wipe away all tears from our eyes and herald in a time when there will be no more pain and suffering, no more darkness – just the glorious Kingdom of God.

INtuitives are also committed to the Jesus who meets people's questions not with pat answers but with further questions thrown back at them. Their approach to Scripture tends to be more symbolic and less literal.

Despite their breadth of vision and their excitement and imagination, Ns run the risk of never stopping to enjoy what is on offer; they can be so busy looking ahead that they fail to appreciate the present moment, and they would do well to take note of Jung's warnings regarding the Extraverted iNtuitive:

> he fritters his life away on things and people, spreading about him an abundance of life which others live and not he himself. In the end he goes away empty.

Thinking spirituality

Thinking spirituality tends to be logical and rational, concerned with matters of truth and justice. The demands of the conscience are very important. The approach to worship and prayer is objective, perhaps even impersonal, and Ts can be alienated by overt shows of friendliness or emotion. It is the Ts, particularly Introverted Ts, who may have most difficulty in sharing the offering of peace during services, and who are most critical of some of the modern hymns and choruses which are so popular in many churches. When an F incumbent asked the whole congregation to join hands during the Lord's Prayer, the Ts in the congregation cringed with embarrassment!

It is important for Ts to act justly, and to hold to truth in the face of opposition. So their prayers may well be about people and situations where there is gross injustice or persecution. For them justice is love incarnate. Thinkers feel concern rather than sympathy, they may well have strong emotions (just as strong as other types) but they are not easily expressed, and they tend to shy away from too emotional forms of spirituality.

They like coherence, order and discipline in their devotional life, and may find that words rather than symbols are important to them. Prayer is faith seeking understanding. They need intelligibility in church services and value well-thought-out preaching. They often have quite a systematic approach to prayer and Bible study, and may well do the latter with the help of commentaries. Thinkers can be the critics within our churches, and one area

163

where they can be heard very often is in expressing the view that the churches are in danger of blurring the distinction between private and public prayer. They tend to the view that public worship is not an appropriate place for 'letting it all hang out'.

St Matthew's Gospel is likely to appeal to them because of its very logical structure – its frontispiece and concluding chapters, and then its five 'books of teaching', reminiscent of the Pentateuch. Within that particular Gospel there is an awareness of law, and God is portrayed as a God of power and might, and the images of the rock and fortress find a resting place within Matthew's Gospel.

It would appear that there are many more Feeling types ordained than Thinking types, and therefore T clergy often find themselves in something of an alien environment, and many of them struggle with this. They take comfort from the fact that there are many more Ts within the secular world, and they are aware of the fact that a great many of them are not attracted by the F spirituality which so many churches promote. The T aspects of God's nature and image are much less likely to be celebrated within churches than the F aspects, and this too means that Ts are often more than a little uneasy within our churches. This is particularly true for T women, who not only have to struggle against the F climate of the churches, but also against the F stereotypes which are placed upon them.

Thinking spirituality is cerebral and objective; it inevitably finds itself being rather defensive, but it is essential for the life and maintenance of the church, for the protection of its doctrine and for the honesty of its concern and integrity. It will never be a popular form, and it will often be misunderstood and even disparaged, but for the Thinking type it is an important and essential aspect of their faith.

Feeling spirituality

The Feeling function makes judgements and decisions based on values, and an F person is one who is particularly concerned about the effect that an action or decision will have upon the other people involved. Feeling is used to develop personal relationships with other people and with God. Chester Michael and Marie Norrisey wrote their book *Prayer and Temperament*[2] following a prayer project conducted throughout 1982 involving 415 participants. They found that 47 per cent of the people taking part were NFs, compared to 32 per cent of SJs, 10.6 per cent NTs and 10.4 per cent SPs – clearly showing the dominance of Fs within the churches. We do not have reliable figures for the UK, but our observations, following many Workshops within the churches, would certainly support the sort of figures that Michael and Norrisey came up with.

Feeling spirituality is personal and subjective, and it yearns for intimacy – both with God and with fellow members of the congregation and other believers. Personal gestures like glances or touch are important to Fs, and for them the offering of a sign of peace provides an ideal opportunity for expressing and receiving love and concern. Feelers can be very vulnerable, and they take upon themselves the blame for disharmony; they can thus identify with the idea and theme of a sinful people who necessitated the death of a loving saviour. They are the sort of people who say 'Sorry!' when someone else bumps into them!

Feelers have a deeply personal spirituality, and the story of the journey to Emmaus resonates with them – 'Did not our hearts burn within us?'. Phrases like: 'The heart has reasons which the mind knows not' are very apposite. Their understanding of God revolves around images such as shepherd, father, mother, bridegroom, faithful husband or wife, and adjectives such as compassionate, good, loving, forgiving. Feelers *know* that God's capacity for forgiveness is infinite.

They want to share their faith in a loving and accepting environment, and the church is seen as a family, and sharing and joy ought to be its obvious characteristics. The I–Thou relationship with God is crucial, and prayer is seen as one of the ways of deepening the intimacy of such a relationship. The story of the Prodigal Son speaks volumes to Fs, and they will tend to focus upon St Luke's Gospel, with its sensitive approach to women and outsiders, and its concern for healing and wholeness.

A sense of value can be noticed in their approach to prayer, which is often 'meditation through intercessory prayer', and shared with others in some form of corporate prayer. There may also be a treasuring of the Eucharist, which emphasizes and symbolizes intimate relationships within the context of the presence of God. Feelers are able to empathize with others, and very often enfold them in their prayers with genuine concern. For many people, this is a very appealing characteristic of the church – 'I didn't know so many people cared' is a familiar comment made by people who have only recently joined a particular congregation.

Feelers (particularly NFs) need to find meaning and significance in their lives, and they want to be assured that whatever they do makes a difference, and that each person has a unique contribution to make. The belief that God has a loving relationship with each individual person and that s/he fits into some overall, harmonious plan – even though s/he may be sinful, or simple – is basic to their understanding of the spiritual life. Feelers need to be assured of this every day, and so daily prayer and quiet are essential, for without it they fade away or dry up like a thirsty plant in a parched land.

This section concludes with words of Gerard Fourez quoted in an article by Robert Repicky:

> Remembering the categories of personalities proposed by Jung, we can see that a good communal celebration will try to provide a variety of symbols so that each type of person can find something to which to relate: there must be silence for the *feelers*, some vision for the *intuitives*, something to understand for the *thinkers*, and something to *do* for the 'pragmatists'.[3]

The less-preferred functions and spirituality

Earlier chapters have explained the theory behind personality type, and have dealt with the dominant and auxiliary functions. The descriptions just covered deal with the spirituality of our dominant functions. Now we also need to explore the effects that our less-preferred (or inferior) functions have upon us. They are normally invisible to others; we tend to keep them subdued, we use them less often and are less at ease with them. But they are part of us, and in a life of discipleship need to be acknowledged and offered to God as part of the offering of our lives.

Some commentators have spoken about 'the self within ourselves' which we try to deny and often hate, because of the discomfort which it causes us. Robert Repicky says of this:

> It is precisely in the realm of the inferior function, where the depth of one's commitment to his relationship with God, in

humble acceptance of himself and desire for transformation, meets the real test. The religious experience of conversion will always be accompanied in some manner by an eruption of the inferior function as it reveals the individual's state of disintegration, rendering him helpless and in need of the healing of God's love and acceptance in grace.[4]

There is debate about terminology in all this; some writers speak about our 'shadow'; others talk of 'inferior functions'; we prefer to use the term 'least preferred' which we feel is less emotive, more neutral and objective. But whatever name we use, we are referring to those functions which are the opposite to our dominant and auxiliary, and indeed, to the whole type profile with its four distinguishing letters. So for the authors, who are ENTP and ENFJ, we are speaking about paying attention to what we can learn from ISFJ and ISTP, and we are particularly concerned with exploring the nature of our least-preferred functions, namely SF and ST.

In our journey to God, the least-preferred functions, those aspects of our personality which we tend to cover up or ignore, occasionally break through and allow us to recognize and accept our imbalance, and move us on towards repentance. Because we tend to repress these parts, they may suddenly break through, and make themselves conspicuous in undesirable ways. This is because we have not learned how to develop them or use them in a sensitive and appropriate manner, and the more a function is repressed the more likely it is to operate independent of our control, manifesting itself in childish or crude ways. A T may be taken by surprise by his or her violent and irrational likes or dislikes which may express themselves in a gushing and unruly manner, an N may be horrified to discover how tempted s/he is by sexual fantasies, and an F type may suddenly break out in a temper and lash out at the people around and express themselves in a cold, cutting and domineering way. Finally, an S operating from his/her least-preferred function may be full of doom and gloom about future possibilities.

Our least-preferred functions therefore reveal the crosses we bear, point out our shallowness, reveal our need for personal growth and our need for integration. We are usually embarrassed, annoyed or hurt when these things are pointed out to us, because we are less adept at handling them. And so our inferior functions

167

are really a two-edged sword; they are necessary for balance, and when worked on can enlarge and enrich our lives, but when repressed can eat away at our soul and suddenly erupt and cause confusion or devastation. When we do use our least-preferred functions they are generally slow and cumbersome and it requires a considerable amount of effort and psychic energy. Very often we find ourselves trapped between our least-preferred and our dominant function which often tries to sabotage or avoid the weaker function by playing to our egocentricity – thus we exaggerate our strengths in an effort to hide our weaknesses, when we really need to be acknowledging and taking control of our least-preferred function.

Michael and Norrisey summarize the situation thus:

> We reach wholeness only when we are willing to engage in the effort and discipline necessary to bring about a working relationship between the Ego (the focal point of our *conscious* life), the shadow (the *unconscious* depths of our inner self), and God. Only when a good partnership between these three is established will we reach the destiny for which we were created. The purpose of daily prayer and meditation is to attain this working relationship.[5]

Personality type and prayer

Among the hundreds of sheets of paper and handouts that we have accumulated over the last few years focusing upon many different aspects of the MBTI, there is one entitled 'Jungian Typology and Tendencies in Prayer' with no date, no authorship nor any other indication of where it came from or who devised it. Another handout, with different typeset, contains exactly the same information! These prompted us to explore the spirituality of type for ourselves and we offer the following as tentative descriptions, with one or two words pointing out where the effects of our less-preferred functions might well need some special care and attention. Because we believe the less-preferred functions are important in shaping our approach to prayer, we are listing each of the functions in their order of preference.

The ISTJ and prayer: Dominant S; Auxiliary T; Third preferred F; Least-preferred N

This type is quiet and serious, dependable and with a tendency towards conservatism. He or she will probably be highly ordered and will have a structured and possibly formal approach to prayer, with a set time being set aside each day. Being an Introvert, time alone with God will be a high priority, and there will be a danger of rigidity in prayer. Time needs to be spent working on iNtuition, seeking more openness and being prepared to accept a wider diversity of outlook and experience than comes naturally. ISTJs like to pray alone, but often find that a regular time of prayer with a trusted group of friends is also meaningful and important to them. It is sometimes difficult for them to express their feelings openly, and keeping a prayer journal might be helpful. They may experience clear answers to prayer, be very conscious of God's loving acceptance and recognize conversion experiences in themselves and others.

Their dominant and auxiliary functions will mean that they are clear-headed, practical and 'earthed' in their praying. Their less-preferred functions suggest that they will need to develop a greater sensitivity towards others, be more generous in their praise and acceptance, and allow their imagination more scope. They should beware, though, of being over-planned and too methodical, and be more prepared for diversity of belief and practice, and to recognize that a lack of structure may not necessarily mean a lack of commitment.

The ISFJ and prayer: Dominant S; Auxiliary F; Third preferred T; Least-preferred N

This type is not too dissimilar to the ISTJ described above. They too will tend to be methodical and may well prefer a set form of prayer. They may have a liking for some of the traditional prayers of the Church, and their devotional life may well centre around specific rituals. This type is often attracted to the ordained ministry. They will have considerable inner strength, and will persevere when their times of prayer seem barren. They are very dependable and have a concern for people, they often have an awareness of history and tradition and, because of their introverted nature, often do not receive the recognition that they deserve.

169

They are strong on commitment to prayer, and are very conscious of their need to give thanks and praise. They are rather quiet in their praying, preferring to pray alone, but may find that in charismatic and other forms of secure and welcoming prayer groups they actually are more forthcoming. They are often conscious of feeling God's presence, and they warm to spiritual experiences, but run the risk of being rather sentimental at times.

Using their less-preferred functions, they could be rather more questioning about their faith and their experiences, and they need to allow their imagination to suggest new possibilities about the ways in which people might believe, pray and experience God in their lives.

Being an Introvert, their auxiliary F is shown to the outer world, which means that they can be exploited more easily than some other types. Their praying needs to recognize this possibility.

The INFJ and prayer: Dominant N; Auxiliary F; Third preferred T; Least-preferred S

INFJs are susceptible to religious experiences, perhaps even mystical experiences, and they place a strong reliance upon their inner life and sense of inner direction. They have a tendency to be individualistic in their approach to prayer, and they may like to be reflective and contemplative in their private devotions. They may well have a broad, inclusive approach and will have a natural concern for people and for human situations. They probably have a dislike for too formal or repeated prayers, and will be unmoved by too many words, much preferring to be left on their own, to explore quietly the inner meanings of prayer and its effectiveness in a world of pain and need.

Symbols and poetry might be of particular value to them, and they might find that keeping a spiritual journal allows them to explore the many dimensions of spirituality. Their exploration will be that of a participant rather than that of an observer.

They may need to be earthed more and to focus upon specific situations and specific people, and they may need to pay more attention to posture and to their own involvement as a person. They may need to work on being rather more tolerant, and they will need to learn how to compromise, and conciliate more. They need to be easier on themselves, give themselves permission to be imperfect, and allow themselves to take time off and not feel guilty about it! Perhaps they need to enjoy life a little more, not be quite so serious – about themselves and their faith and life in general.

INTJ and prayer: Dominant N; Auxiliary T; Third preferred F; Least-preferred S

The INTJ is probably the most self-confident of all the types. They are decisive and can be quite single-minded, much preferring their own inner direction rather than being directed by others. They are prone to introspection, can be rather stubborn and self-opinionated and dislike small-talk and casual conversation. They are high achievers, and bring to their devotional life the same competence and single-mindedness that they apply to the rest of their life.

They need a considerable amount of time for their private prayer, and this is probably well organized. They will prefer praying in silence, and prefer to be alone. They are open to mystical experience, which will serve to reinforce their own devotion but may not be passed on to others very easily or illuminate the corporate body. Being an NT they may explore many different types of prayer, and probably will have logically assessed their suitability to their own temperament.

This type may need to work on being open and more passive in prayer – that is, relaxing their T and allowing themselves to 'feel' and experience the presence of God. They will need to allow themselves to be more relaxed and less organized in their approach, and pay more attention to the present moment, allowing themselves to relax and enjoy God rather more. They will find informality and spontaneity difficult to cope with, and may have to work hard at finding ways of sharing prayer with others. They will also have to work at recognizing the reality and activity of God in the outside world of people and activities, particularly in situations which appear to be illogical or chaotic.

The ISTP and prayer: Dominant T; Auxiliary S; Third preferred N; Least-preferred F

This type is usually quite reserved and objective, but also practical and efficient. ISTPs will have a no-nonsense approach to prayer: they will have thought it out and found it to be supportive and useful in their lives. Being active people, they will want to be able to say their prayers as they go about their daily business, and will find meaning in exploring the idea of the 'practice of the presence of God'. They will experience God in the ordinary events of daily life and may be drawn to a spirituality of contemplation to be set alongside practical activities such as gardening or walking. They will have used their thinking to explore possible types of prayer, and may well have read books on prayer or attended workshops. They may have sought some form of guidance and will be more likely to be following a pattern which has been suggested to them which they have found relevant than to have explored differing forms themselves.

They may need to allow themselves to be more open to the needs of other people, and to wait upon others. They may have a tendency to be impatient, and perhaps need to develop a friendship with a trusted person with whom they can talk about prayer and learn about other people's experiences. They could try and co-operate with others more and to allow themselves room for new insights which may not appear to have much practical relevance.

The ISFP and prayer: Dominant F; Auxiliary S; Third preferred N; Least-preferred T

ISFPs enjoy prayer: it is a liberating experience for them, often Spirit-filled, and can be expressed with music and colour and movement. They can feel things very deeply and are often artistic and members of close-knit prayer groups or congregations. They are open to charismatic worship, and can feel stultified by too much insistence on tradition or formalism.

ISFPs expect to develop a deep and personal experience of God, and their prayer life is a voluntary and spontaneous response to that experience. They recognize specific answers to prayer, and they are attracted to specific actions, such as the laying on of hands, or the posture of their body in prayer. They lay special emphasis on thanksgiving and rejoicing.

They may need to develop a more consistent approach to prayer, and be more open to the critical reservations of others. Although they are spontaneous and flexible, they may need to allow their iNtuition to suggest different approaches, and they also need to allow other people to travel along different paths – recognizing that their own understanding and approach will not be appropriate for everyone. They may need perseverance in prayer, and to operate on a broader canvas and include in their prayers subjects and concerns which are rather less tangible or immediate. Perhaps a piece of theological study might be taken on as a prayerful activity.

The INFP and prayer: Dominant F; Auxiliary N; Third preferred S; Least-preferred T

Prayer is extremely important to INFPs, and they spend a great deal of time alone in prayer. They may read widely about its practice, have lots of books about different types of prayer, and spend a lot of time in quietness, meditation and spontaneous prayers of gratitude and thanksgiving. Having a dominant F, they may well have shared prayer with others, and may belong to one or more prayer groups. Their N, however, may make them feel that all such groups fail to satisy them and in the end they will find consolation in private, personal prayer. They often have a strong sense of God's presence with them, and this is deeply meaningful and central to their lives. In prayer, they can be themselves before God in a way in which they cannot be themselves before anyone else.

They may not follow liturgical texts too closely, preferring to explore new and different forms. They expect to have and to enjoy a deep sense of God's presence with them. They often have 'hunches' about what they should do, and they may well have vivid dreams to which they pay particular attention.

There is a danger that they become too introverted and self-centred in their prayers and they need to explore ways in which they might extravert themselves more, and also discover ways of using their Thinking in their prayers. They may find it helpful to explore different liturgical texts, and to focus their minds upon some specific situations. They could try praying about structural or political themes without always personalizing the issues, and recognize that there may be times when difficult decisions have to be taken and pain borne in ways which may not seem immediately consistent with discipleship.

The INTP and prayer: Dominant T; Auxiliary N; Third preferred S; Least-preferred F

INTPs are often intelligent, tending towards theory, self-contained and with little room for idle talk and socializing. Their prayers are personal, solitary, conceptual and quiet. They may find it difficult to share feelings and will not naturally be at home in prayer groups. They may find classical texts helpful, and may well have explored some of the great traditional forms of prayer. Their praying can take the form of 'dialogues with theological figures', and they need to have time and space to develop and concentrate their praying. Without the necessary conditions, they are able to abandon their prayers until the conditions are available; in deferring their prayers they rest upon their knowledge and understanding of the greatness of God and the fact that they are sustained by God whether they pray or not; their spiritual life depends upon God's faithfulness not theirs.

With a highly developed T and a poorly developed F they can have difficulty in expressing emotion, and there is always the danger that their prayers become abstract almost to the point of being a continuation of study. They may have difficulty in sharing experiences of prayer, and in teaching or developing ideas about prayer in ways which others can easily understand and relate to.

They may need to concentrate on making their prayers more person-centred, and more earthed in day-to-day situations. They may also need to pay more attention to music and colour and to the length and content of their prayers. When involved in public worship, they may have difficulty in sharing in the prayers of others, or in leading prayers in such a way as to involve and engage others.

The ESTP and prayer: Dominant S; Auxiliary T; Third Preferred F; Least-preferred N

ESTPs are pragmatists: men and women of action, concerned with the here-and-now, and as such their approach to prayer is more 'matter of fact' and functional. They are not likely to spend a long time in prayer, and when they do pray it is likely to be concerned with practical matters which relate to their everyday experiences. They are likely to be unimpressed by mysticism or by deep interior searching, but may find the immediacy of charismatic worship speaks to them. They are likely to rely on others to provide the prayers, and are happy for other types to do the praying while they get on with the doing! They may find music, particularly well-known hymns, a help and may be able to use the structure and words of the hymns as a basis for their prayers.

ESTPs are helped by belonging to a lively congregation and many of them also find that prayer groups assist them in their devotions. They are not very fond of long periods of silence, nor of praying on their own. They might find books of prayers helpful, and often will find a way into prayer from reading passages from the Bible.

There is a danger that their prayers get stuck in a simplistic rut, and they may well need help in developing an appreciation of their own inner life. They could try to concentrate upon issues and situations and remember the people who are involved in them, and hold them before God. ESTPs need to recognize that their work and activity can also be part of their prayer life, and they may find that several short times of quiet and reflection throughout the day are more appropriate than one long time in the morning or evening.

The ESFP and prayer: Dominant S; Auxiliary F; Third Preferred T; Least-preferred N

People of this type tend to be very popular; they are good communicators, good fun and natural leaders. They bring this gregariousness into their spiritual life, and are evident in prayer groups and in leading worship, particularly with young people and in less formal situations. They may be drawn to charismatic worship, or enjoy visual aids, music or a variety of external stimuli. They may well prefer the occasional burst of high-intensity prayer to the ongoing, formalized structure preferred by some other types. Thus special rallies, or all-night vigils or weekend conferences may mean more to them, as they can engage their whole selves in such activities, and worship God with their personalities and their activities, as well as with their mind and heart.

ESFPs expect to receive clear answers to their prayers; they look for miracles and are not disappointed. They tend not to be over-impressed by logic and the minutiae of theological discussion and prefer a practical and straightforward approach to faith. They can find healing services and devotions dealing with suffering and brokenness particularly meaningful.

They need to spend time reflecting upon the richness of Christian tradition and allowing themselves to be open to experiences which are not their own. They may also need to develop a larger time-perspective and learn how to 'rest in God' without needing to be active and personally involved in everything.

175

The ENFP and prayer: Dominant N; Auxiliary F; Third Preferred T; Least-preferred S

ENFPs tend to be imaginative, friendly, and enthusiastic, and they bring these qualities to their spiritual life. They are often unconventional and do not always find the traditional patterns and approaches of the church meaningful. They are not overkeen on routine and small details – preferring instead a wide and flexible approach – and they can become impatient with too great an emphasis on routine.

They are unlikely to spend long periods in silence or in solitary prayer, and will find shorter, intense periods of prayer more congenial – especially when linked to a particular person or crisis. Their natural warmth and interest in people means that their prayers can be very supportive of others, and they will tend to identify with the subject of their prayer, sharing in the pain or joy of the situation. Their dominant iNtuition means that they grasp possibilities, and being Perceivers they are flexible and open-ended. This, together with their auxiliary Feeling means that they can have a sense of the authenticity of their spiritual journey, even though it may not follow conventional lines.

As they grow older they may need to explore less, and be happier settling into a more patterned form of prayer, and they may wish to become rather more reflective and less active.

The ENTP and prayer: Dominant N; Auxiliary T; Third preferred F; Least-preferred S

ENTPs are always looking for a challenge, they want to discover new and ingenious ways of doing things and they dislike routine and convention. They like broad, overall sweeps, disliking detail, and these tendencies form the basis of their spiritual formation. They get bored with routine patterns of prayer quickly, and only really come alive when there is something new and challenging on the horizon.

They are self-critical, and often wonder if they pray at all, with their T forever raising doubts and their N always looking for new possibilities. They can enjoy exploring new dimensions of prayer but these need to be contemporary and not just new to them. That is, they can become bored with exploring traditional or classic forms of spirituality. They are open to the idea of giving time to prayer, and may enjoy the use of music, but they are always ready to admit that they have moved away from prayer into something else as the time passes!

ENTPs need to pay more attention to detail, and to be more aware of the present realities rather than future possibilities. They may find it difficult to experience personal satisfaction in prayer, and should be prepared to 'stick with it' rather than give up. They need to be less self-deprecating about the authenticity of their spiritual life.

The ESTJ and prayer: Dominant T; Auxiliary S; Third preferred N; Least-preferred F

ESTJs are loyal, dependable, realistic, and good organizational people, very often in leadership positions. Their spirituality is also loyal and dependable, consistent and fairly conservative. They have tried the well-worn path of the saints and found it sustaining, and they have little desire to seek alternatives. They usually find that the traditional forms serve them well, and they are more concerned with being active in the world, supported and undergirded by their prayers rather than expending their energy on their interior life. They are respectful of tradition, and like their prayers to be well-organized and structured. They may well have set times, and often use a prayer diary or prayer lists to ensure that they 'cover the ground' and do not let their personal likes and dislikes dictate the content of their prayers too much.

They appreciate praying with others, but like it to be structured, preferring the worship of the liturgy to spontaneous prayer meetings. Their personal prayer is disciplined, and once they have come to the end of it they are unlikely to spend extra time in silence and inner exploration.

They may need to allow themselves to be more open and flexible, and to believe that they are not letting themselves or God down if they occasionally miss a time of prayer, or if they use an alternative form of prayer. They need to ensure that there are times of warmth and sensitivity in the content of their prayer, and they need to allow themselves to live with uncertainty and a sense of the provisional. Occasionally they could let other people direct their praying and thinking, and loosen their grip on the controls!

The ESFJ and prayer: Dominant F; Auxiliary S; Third preferred N; Least-preferred T

This is perhaps the most sociable and gregarious of all the types;

they are outgoing, friendly and relate easily, they are also caring and seek harmony. It is not surprising, therefore, that they tend to see prayer as sharing a friendship with God, it is relaxed and confident. They may well enjoy music and may be open to charismatic worship. They will be at home within structured forms of congregational worship and easily relate to prayer groups. They may have fairly strong principles which influence their prayers, giving them a sense of direction and clarity about specifics. ESFJs tend to play down difficulties and dislike facing up to conflict, and so their prayers have a tendency to stress harmony, peace and the overall unity of humankind.

They may often experience times of joy and peace in their prayers, and like many other Extraverts, they see their life of prayer as supporting their life of action, which is the principal sphere of their discipleship.

There will be a tendency for ESFJs to shy away from intellectual rigour if this might mean disagreeing with others, and they may need to find ways of engaging their mind in their prayers rather more often. They are also prone to get bogged down in specifics, and may need to be reminded of the grandeur and majesty and holiness of God.

The ENFJ and prayer: Dominant F; Auxiliary N; Third preferred S; Least-preferred T

ENFJs are natural leaders in groups, and people look to them for support and guidance. They have a warmth and an openness to people which also characterize their prayers. They seldom experience anguish in prayer, but rather are able to relax in the knowledge of their acceptance by God. Whilst not given to prolonged periods of silence or contemplation (because as Extraverts, they find that experiences with people in the world are their principal reminders of God), they can nevertheless appreciate the place of silence and solitude rather more than ENTPs and ENTJs.

They are often good at leading worship, having the ability to combine social activism and a concern for the world with a sense of detachment and an awareness of God's presence and healing power. They are inclined to find traditional prayer rather restricting, but do not necessarily rebel against it. They are willing to accept the many varieties of prayer and religious experience that other people present them with, and have an inclusive and broad approach to spirituality.

As Thinking is their least preferred function, they tend not to agonize over prayer, or analyse it or argue about it – although when they do address some of the real problems raised by prayer, they are often able to explore the issues with honesty, expressing their doubts, but all within the context of their assurance of God's love and acceptance. Their general rather laid-back approach can have overtones of laziness, and they need to be aware of the fact that there is a place for struggle within prayer! There is also a place for specifics, and ENFJs need to ensure that their prayers do not become too generalized.

The ENTJ and prayer: Dominant T; Auxiliary N; Third Preferred S; Least-preferred F

ENTJs are highly dependable, organized and logical. They are often found in leadership positions, and they fit easily into bureaucratic structures. This same pattern of orderliness and resistance to change replicates itself in their prayer life. They are likely to value the well-tried-and-tested forms of prayer and spirituality of the church, and those forms of prayer that they learned when they were younger. They are suspicious of, and resistant to, too much emotion in prayer, and they tend to dislike experimental liturgies and changes within the normal way of doing things. They respect tradition.

They are often good at leading public worship, bringing to it dignity, a sense of calmness and an awareness of centuries of Christian tradition. They have an assurance about the faithfulness and dependability of God, and approach their prayers with a sense of duty and an awareness of the majesty and sovereignty of God. They are unlikely to spend a great deal of time in silent or in solitary prayer.

They could benefit from becoming rather less tied to formal patterns and forms of prayer, and allow rather more specific subjects to be mentioned and focused upon. They also need to work at allowing their prayers to be more person-centred, recognizing the friendship of God and the possibilities for healing and restoration of those who are broken. Flexibility may well be a problem, and they need to allow themselves to experience different forms of worship, different kinds of music and to be open to the possibility of different kinds of religious experience.

179

Conclusion

John Biersdorf, Dean and President of the Ecumenical Theological Center, Detroit has explored the variety of ways in which clergy pray, and in his book *How Prayer Shapes Ministry*, says:

> Prayer images hover around the central silence of God. At times of grace they may become irrelevant and sink into imageless communion with Spirit, returning as attention wanders and the habitual chatter of the mind returns. We tend to pray the same way we live, embedded in our scripts – our accustomed patterns of living and coping. These habitual choices of fear and love are most often the agenda for prayer. We arrive in the presence of God wearing them; unwitting or intentionally, we ask for their transformation from fear to love. In a sense they are the posthypnotic suggestions left by our parents and teachers and the circumstances of our history – suggestions to feel, think, image, and act in stereotyped ways. Consciously aware of only some of the patterns, we bring them all to God to be transformed in love.[6]

The way we are is the way we pray, and it is important that we do not feel pressurized into feeling that someone else's spiritual journey and experiences should be ours. Extraverts, in particular, need help and encouragement to recognize that their path of discipleship takes them through the world of activity, and that their experiences in the world can well become their prayers.

In reading through the type descriptions and prayer given in this chapter it is helpful to look also at how the opposite type to you approaches prayer, and if you belong to a secure and accepting group, it could be a very useful exercise to sit and talk through these matters with your opposite type (recognizing that the Extraverts will probably have to take the lead!).

For those who want to do further reading you might well find Gordon Jeff's two books *Spiritual Direction for Every Christian* and *Am I still a Christian: Twenty Questions about your Spiritual Direction* a considerable help, and Lawrence and Diana Osborn have a chapter on 'Personalities in Prayer' in their book *God's Diverse People*. Michael and Norrisey's book, *Prayer and Temperament* mentioned earlier approaches the subject very much from within the tradition of the Roman Catholic Church, and whilst this is one of the most substantial works available on personality and prayer written from the perspective of type and temperament, not everyone will immediately feel conversant with the traditions of Benedictine, Augustinian, Franciscan, Thomistic and Ignatian spirituality.

As with so much of the Myers Briggs Indicator, we can finish with words of hope! It is all right to be the person that you are; you will undoubtedly have gifts and insights which others do not have, and you will also need to share in and appreciate the gifts of others. This is as true in the area of prayer as it is in other areas. The message is clear: recognize and accept and value the gifts and insights that you have; work on understanding just why and how some situations and some people are more difficult to understand and appreciate than others, and learn to value and accept the gifts that others bring. God has created a rich diversity, and the particular characteristics that make us ourselves (rather than someone else) are all part of the richness of creation. Honour, value, respect and cherish this diversity, and offer to God the person that you really are, rather than the person you feel that you ought to be, should be, or want to be!

Part Four

11 A Bit of Fun for Christmas!

How many people spend hours and hours each year as November moves towards December wondering what on earth they can buy for Uncle Jim, Aunt Ethel, the next door neighbour and the person who feeds the dog? Perhaps an understanding of type might help! This was certainly the view of the Editor of *The Type Reporter* in 1988 and 1989 when the journal ran articles on just that topic[1]. We have run a similar exercise in several of our Workshops, asking people to explore the area of gifts from the perspective of type and temperament and the results are not only fun, but also illuminating. It really does make sense to ask yourselves questions about the personality of your aunt or uncle before you start worrying about their present.

And the way that people view Christmas itself can be affected by their type and temperament – which may explain why some members of the family are less enthusiastic about it than others, and why, what should be a time of rejoicing, can be for some a time of considerable tension.

Types and Christmas

The Sensing–Perceivers

The SPs enjoy the present moment, they tend to be fun-loving and active people, so for them Christmas can be a time of high spirits and holiday. They are more likely to be the people who go away for the holiday, either abroad to ski, or to some luxury hotel so that they can spoil themselves. They will almost certainly want to go out, whether they Christmas at home or not. A long brisk walk, or some form of organized sport; one thing is for sure, they will not want to sit around the television in front of a big fire for days on end!

They may wish the Festival to be child-centred, knowing that they themselves are also children, and they get a great deal of pleasure from giving and receiving lots of presents. They prefer several small presents to one big one, and take great delight in wrapping them up so that they look good, and they also receive considerable tactile pleasure when unwrapping parcels. They also like surprises, so don't tell them beforehand what you are thinking of giving them!

Sensing–Perceivers may well make their own presents – painting a picture, carving some wood or knitting a garment – and they get considerable satisfaction from putting something of 'themselves' into their gift.

Choosing a present for an SP is much easier when you remember that they enjoy their senses, and so anything which has to do with sight, sound, smell, taste or touch is likely to be on the right lines. Think in terms of a picture, a beautiful calendar, a book with lots of photographs or even a collection of photographs of them when they were younger. Check out their musical tastes and think in terms of a record, tape or compact disc, or a ticket to the theatre, a concert or a pop festival. Food and drink are always acceptable, and SPs more than any other temperament are likely to enjoy the special marmalade or jam, the box of chocolates or bottle of wine. A meal-out voucher for two, or a special flower arrangement which fills the house with fragrance are other possibilities. There are now so many opportunities to pander to the body, and SPs particularly will delight in body oils, various sorts of 'smellies' and those special extravagances which they may not succumb to on a day by day basis. If they live in a city, see if there is a flotation tank, and buy them a voucher for that.

The key to reaching the heart of an SP is to activate their senses, allow them to enjoy themselves, and to do something in the present moment. Sporting gear is usually acceptable, as SPs tend to be outdoor types and keen on sport. They also have a great many DIY enthusiasts in their number, and so the odd drill or plane or selection of nails and screws may not go amiss! Whatever you get them, wrap it up well and make it look interesting. Even a voucher or token can be put in a box for a surprise!

The iNtuitive–Thinkers

If SPs are full of excitement and looking for ways of celebrating, NTs can appear to be diametrically opposed to them! NTs often find the Christmas period quite difficult, they place themselves outside the situation and observe what is happening, and can come up with rather caustic observations. They see people running round in ever decreasing circles, getting tired and frenzied, spending inordinate amounts of money on what are often seen to be useless gifts, and they tend to become over-critical and detached. They are often wearied by what they perceive as family traditions, with their repetitive nature, and they feel forced to join in, and often do so grudgingly. NTs often find holidays a problem at the best of times, and so very often they find the Christmas holiday particularly difficult.

Possible ways through these difficulties are to enlist the support of NTs at the planning stage, and persuade or invite them to contribute to the thinking at an early stage. Perhaps suggest that each year something new could be explored, and encourage them to share their ideas about what would be appealing if the normal traditions were not slavishly followed. Remember, NTs need to use their Intuition to see new possibilities, and they need to check these possibilities out via a process of rational thinking. It may even be possible to encourage them to forego their intellectual-ism, just for a few days, and join in the fun – but they may need prior warning of this idea, so that they have time to think about it!

INtuitive-Thinkers lay great stress upon competence, and buying presents for other people can be a considerable strain for them as they have to find the *perfect* gift for each person, and it is often their failure to be able to do this that triggers off their general dislike of the whole process. They may need help in buying presents, especially from people who can be excited by the process.

The NT temperament is perhaps the most difficult one to buy presents for. They tend to be rather bookish people, and that may be a safe route to take. Book tokens seldom give the giver a great deal of pleasure, but they can be very acceptable as a gift for an NT as it then allows him or her to go off and use their N in exploring all the possible types of book that they might buy. In any case, they like browsing in bookshops and this gives them the perfect excuse. They often like things on a global scale, and so photographs from space, an Atlas or map book or something which relates to the universe might be along the right lines. As an NT myself, I have gained enormous pleasure from two fluor-escent photographs – one of the moon and the other of the earth from space – a pleasure which most of my friends find difficult to understand!

Think through their relaxation times and see if there is

anything that can add to them. But beware, being a T they may have quite specific views. If they are interested in music, a record or compact disc would be a good idea, but it is probably better to talk through with them just which recording they would like: it is no good giving them Pavarotti's *Tosca* when they actually wanted Tito Gobi's version! NTs are not very concerned about surprises and secrets, and so you will not be spoiling it for them if you check things out beforehand – or if you give them their present after Christmas; in fact, many NTs won't mind if you don't give them a present at all!

The Sensing–Judgers

These are the early planners, the people who begin working on Christmas as soon as their summer holiday is over. They may already have bought their cards and some of their presents in the January sales! By the beginning of December they have probably worked out all their presents, their menu and their guests; their cupboards and freezer will already be well stocked and they will have a clear idea of how they will spend each day of the holiday. SJs prefer to give hospitality rather than receive it, because that way they know that everything will be in order and everything will work out according to their plan and wishes. They may well entertain a great deal and their home is often full of people – even when SJs are isolated and alone, they fill their minds with memories of people and Christmases past.

Tradition is all-important for SJs. They like things to be the same as they were last year, and the year before . . . right back to their childhood days in fact. Certain people have certain tasks to do, and they are done in pre-determined ways, and on pre-determined days. It is important for them that the past is remembered and maintained, and that they pass a living tradition on to their children. They may not always be good at delegating because that means losing control, and the end result may not be exactly what they had in mind, or it may deviate from the normal way of doing things and that brings uncertainty and breaks the tradition. SJs are strong on emphasizing the family unit, and so it is important that families come together for Christmas, and celebrate their shared history.

It is easier to understand the tensions that sometimes occur in families when they are made up of SJs and NTs when this knowledge of type and temperament is brought to bear on situations: Should the Christmas tree always stand there? Couldn't someone else decorate it for a change? Do we have to go for drinks to the Browns on Christmas Eve every year?

Buying presents for SJs can be quite difficult as they have a keen sense of what is appropriate. More than any other temperament they have an innate sense of what should or should not be given and so the giver always labours under a sense of judgement! It helps to remember that SJs tend to be responsible people, holding responsible positions within their workplace, within the community or within the family, and so anything that allows them to operate more effectively, more efficiently or more pleasurably might be worth exploring. A decent fountain pen or propelling pencil, some form of stationery or equipment, a decent calendar or diary . . . these are the things that 'speak' to an SJ, but they need to be appropriate, and they need to be reliable. A blotchy pen, a diary with insufficient space (or too much space) or a piece of useless office equipment may be received with a smile and put away or thrown away very promptly! When you hit upon the right thing though, it will give great pleasure and be used for years and years, and commented on and treasured.

Bear in mind that Js like completion, and so think about whether they are collectors of any sort – silver spoons? coins? stamps? porcelain dishes? Is there anything that you can give which will add to their collection, and bring a sense of completion or fulfilment? Perhaps build up a tradition of giving them a particular annual – Wisden, the Bedside Guardian, the latest Giles – something that reminds them that you always give them that particular thing (though ensure that they really like it, there is nothing worse than getting a gardening annual every year if you can't stand gardening!). A good family photograph in a nice frame is a good idea for elderly relatives or for people who live a long way away, and most parents always like to have photographs of their children, and grandchildren.

Don't feel deflated if SJs don't 'ooze' over your present – they are unlikely to do so, even if it is just what they really wanted. They are more likely to take everything in their stride, and are unlikely to show overmuch emotion whether the gift be wonderful or awful; the important thing is that you remembered to give them something!

The iNtuitive–Feelers

The Christmas message is at the heart of the NF – Peace on earth and goodwill to all humankind. There is so much about Christmas that affirms the NF, which speaks to their condition, and which affirms what they value most. It is therefore strange that sometimes this temperament can feel most disappointed with the festival and holiday; it is almost as though it promises so much, has such potential, that it is almost impossible for it to live up to it all. The NF will see all the work that has gone into the preparation, will see all that has been done and spent and given and received, and yet sometimes feel that the real, authentic intimacy has somehow eluded the whole process.

They can often escape into fantasy at Christmastime: NFs can allow their N to have freedom and imagine a world which really was changed by peace, in which people really did care for one another, and in which the meek were allowed to stand up and be counted. Their F and N can be fulfilled, but then they realize that reality isn't exactly like that, and they become aware of the great gap between life as it is and life as it might be.

Finding presents for NFs can tax the ingenuity of most people, for how can you find something that is intimate, meaningful, full of harmony and which also brings fulfilment? What you have to remember is that it is the personal contact that matters most, it is the fact that you have cared sufficiently to remember them. The more personal that you can make the gift the more likely it is that you will succeed in pleasing them: photographs illustrating your relationship, pictures of a place where you have shared good times, or music which brings back shared memories. If they are interested in books, something which explores inner depths, or which tells the story of the triumph of someone overcoming adversity. If you can find something which demonstrates why their relationship to you is important, that is ideal.

If all else fails, give an NF something which is really important to you, and which you would love to have, and tell them that you wanted to share this special gift with them. The greatest gift that you can give to NFs is your appreciation, so try to find ways of letting them know why you like them and what they mean to you.

Christmas services

More people go to church services at Christmas than at any other time of the year, and an understanding of type and temperament should be a help to those responsible for planning the worship. Ideally, churches should try to cater for the expectations and needs of the different temperaments: SPs will want fun, spontaneity and good visual and musical stimuli; NTs will want their minds stretched, to explore if there is any real substance behind all the myths. They will want new angles on old issues, and will appreciate not being automatically involved in what they might perceive as rather artificial joviality; SJs will need the tradition – same old carols, in the same order, with the same nativity play – they probably would be quite content with the same old sermon as well; NFs will want to immerse themselves in the meaning of Christmas, and they will want to drink in its spirit to the full; renewing their vision of peace and goodwill is of enormous importance and they will feed on it for a long time to come. How churches are to hold this mix together is a task demanding skill, sensitivity, planning and good publicity – but it is worth having a go at trying to meet the differing needs and expectations.

12 Two Remarkable Women

Several years ago I watched a television programme in which the comedians Morecambe and Wise fooled around with the musician André Previn. Eric Morecambe played the piano during the first movement of Grieg's piano concerto, at least he tried to play the first few bars of the concerto. It was brought to a quick stop by Previn who could not bear the soloist's ham-fisted vamping. When he tackled Eric Morecambe about playing wrong notes, the comedian retorted that he wasn't playing the wrong notes, he was playing the right notes, but in the wrong order! I was reminded of this when reading of an incident in the early life of Isabel Briggs, an incident which gave some hint of the innovative powers of thought which, years later, were to produce the Myers Briggs Type Indicator (MBTI). It happened in 1903 when she was just six years old and was taking a long train journey across America to visit her grandfather in California. In order to pass the time away, she pretended to be a librarian and after one of the passengers had asked for a particular book she went away and returned in a few minutes with an imaginary book and said: 'We don't have that one, but this is a dictionary and it has all the same words in it'. This delightful story is but one of many which occurs in the very readable biography of Isabel Myers and her mother Katharine Briggs *Katharine and Isabel: Mother's Light, Daughter's Journey* written by Frances Wright Saunders.[1]

It is important to remember that what might, at first acquaintance, appear to be rather detached, impersonal sheets – the raw materials for taking the MBTI – actually have a history behind them, a history which involves laughter and tears, hopes and fears, and which embraces the lives of people and which is forever interwoven with their own stories and life experiences.

The MBTI takes its name from the two women who designed it, and for whom it became an abiding passion and the culmination of over 50 years' thought and work. Katharine Elizabeth Cook was born in Michigan in January 1875; she went to Michigan Agricultural College where she met the man who was to become her husband at the end of 1896. Their first child, Isabel was born the following year and two years later they had a son who died before his second birthday. A very close bond was forged between mother and daughter, intensified by the fact that Isabel was educated at home for most of her childhood by a mother who had very advanced views on education and child-rearing, views which were published over the years in various articles. Isabel was extremely bright and, as a child, had some of her writing published. She was inquisitive and was encouraged to ask questions which her parents always tried to answer truthfully, Katharine was to write, about that time: 'It is not what a child knows that makes him clever; it is his attitude toward what he does not know'.

In September 1915 Isabel entered Swarthmore College and began a highly successful academic career, and it was there that she met and fell in love with Clarence Gates ('Chief') Myers a law student, whom she married in 1918. Her mother, Katharine, had ambitions to become a writer and she was particularly interested in exploring the personality of characters; she used to read biographies a great deal and try to find some way of categorizing the various people. She was particularly taken by this young man who had entered her daughter's life, feeling that she had never come across his type of personality before. Both parents were delighted with their new son-in-law and there developed a mutual respect and affection that was to last for the remainder of their lives.

In 1923 Katharine read Carl Jung's book *Psychological Types* and felt that this provided exactly the sort of theoretical structure which made sense of the work that she had been doing, and she corresponded with Jung for the next decade and more before meeting him in New York in 1937.

Meanwhile Isabel and her husband were setting up home and establishing themselves in a career. There were attempts to begin a family which brought great sadness following a stillborn birth and then the death of a baby daughter, but eventually the birth of a son and then a daughter brought intense joy and satisfaction to the whole family. Katharine continued to supply Isabel with her radical views on childrearing, and both mother and daughter had various articles printed.

It would be difficult to exaggerate the closeness of the relationship between mother and daughter. Very often they wrote each other daily letters, exchanging views on a whole manner of subjects, but particularly about education and childrearing, and the differing types of people that they met and read about. One such exchange gives a good example, coming as it did when they were discussing Isabel's engagement and the problems relating to the question of whose responsibility it was to tell people: Katharine wrote:

> It is the PRIVILEGE of parents of grown up children to make suggestions; and it is the DUTY of the children to give serious consideration to those suggestions. It is the PRIVILEGE of grown up children to make their own decisions; and it is the DUTY of the parents to respect and acquiesce in these decisions.[2]

Both mother and daughter had an aptitude for writing, and in 1926 Katharine had an article published in *The New Republic*. 'Meet Yourself' was an article about personality type and was regarded as very avant-garde. A couple of years later she published an article about education, and using her theories about different types said that to train children in the same way was like 'sending the goldfish to school with the canary'.

In 1928, in response to an advertised competition, Isabel wrote a mystery/detective novel and was delighted to win the prize of $7,500. *Murder Yet to Come* beat off some formidable competition including a novel by the originator of the Perry Mason series! This was a major achievement and the book was translated into many different languages. The publishers were eager to sign her up on a contract for an annual novel. Isabel wanted to try her hand at writing plays though, but her play *Death Calls for Margin* never made the same impact as her novel did.

It was not until the war came that she really began to settle down and begin working seriously on the ideas which her mother had kept writing and talking about, and in 1943 her husband, Chief, registered a copyright for what would eventually become the Briggs Myers Type Indicator. It would be several years later before the order of the names was reversed. From that time on, with her children growing up and developing distinguished careers of their own, the Indicator became her abiding passion.

It was not easy for an unqualified woman to break into the psychological establishment in America, and the next 30 years tell the story of her struggles against prejudice, her amazing stamina as she worked revising and revising the questions and the questionnaire time and time again. And she had to learn the skill of statistics, and all this before computers were available – indeed, it was a great step forward when she was able to transfer to a desk top hand calculator. In 1953 she was able to give the test to 3,605 students and in 1964 began the Myers Longitudinal Survey of over 10,000 nursing students.

It was her sheer tenacity and ability which enabled her to 'hang-in' when confronted by rebuff after rebuff from so many in the academic and psychological establishment. An interesting insight into her character is given in a confidential memo written by a critical colleague to the Head of the Educational Testing Service under whose auspices the Indicator was being developed at that time. He wrote:

> Mrs Myers has dedicated her life and that of her family to the concept of type; she believes it to be a profound and extremely important social discovery. She believes her Indicator provides the way to make this concept useful in educational and vocational guidance, marital and vocational adjustment, elaboration and diagnoses, and therapy of personality problems, etc. She is bright, energetic, compulsive, and very persistent. Anything that may further the development and promulgation of the Indicator and its acceptance by the professional public transcends any other code of behavior. The woman has worked day and night for ... (many) years with this goal overriding all other personal goals; she is a kind of modern Joan of Arc, and her cause is as sacred; she simply doesn't anticipate being trapped and bound at the stake.[3]

In 1975 the Consulting Psychologists Press took over the publication of the Indicator and from that moment it took off. Even so, the Director was surprised to find that Isabel insisted on being involved in all matters relating to the nature of the typescript used and every indentation in the text; he had to reach some form of gentle mutual agreement that they should each stick to the things that they had expertise in, for, after all, it was in the best interest of both of them that the Indicator became as widely used as possible!

She said that the whole Indicator project was 'the result of four pieces of tremendous good luck' – the fact that she had a research scientist for a father, a college-trained creative woman for her mother, an unusual and utterly supportive husband, and the fact that Jung published *Psychological Types* at just the time when her mother was working on a similar theory.

At the age of 78, with several years of coping with cancer behind her, and after several operations, she gave a paper entitled 'Making the Most of Individual Gifts' at the first National MBTI Conference. She was in her early 80s when, together with her son Peter, she worked on the basic textbook explaining the Indicator – *Gifts Differing* – and was able to correct the proofs shortly before she died; sadly, though, she never saw its actual publication.

Her book takes its title from words in St Paul's letter to the Romans, and it was words from one of Paul's other letters (1 Corinthians) which were read at her funeral in 1980: 'Now there are varieties of gifts, but the same Spirit'.

The cover of *Katharine and Isabel* says: 'This then, is the story of two very remarkable women and their families, of the powerful bond between mother and daughter, and how they faced devastating personal tragedies and still left a stunning legacy of achievement.' We can only agree.

NOTES

Chapter 1
1. I. Briggs Myers, *Gifts Differing*. Consulting Psychologists Press Inc., Palo Alto, CA. (1980, 1990). Obtainable from Oxford Psychologists Press, 311–321 Banbury Road, Oxford OX2 7JH (tel: 0865 510 203).

Chapter 4
1. W. Zimmerman, *Make Beliefs*. Guarionex Press Ltd., New York (1987).

Chapter 5
1. D. Keirsey and M. Bates, *Please Understand Me: Character and Temperament Type* (1978). Obtainable from Oxford Psychologists Press.
2. O. Kroeger and J. Thuesen, *Type Talk*. Tilden Press, Delta Books (1988), p. 52. Obtainable from Oxford Psychologists Press.

Chapter 6
1. J. Provost, 'You don't fight fair' in *The Type Recorder* vol. 3, no. 3. Obtainable from 524 North Paxton Street, Alexandria, VA. 22304 (1988) and from Oxford Psychologists Press.
2. I. Briggs Myers, *Gifts Differing*, p. 135.

Chapter 7
1. J. Provost, *The Type Reporter*, vol 3, nos 9–12 and vol 4, nos 1–3 (1989).
2. S. Krebs Hirsh and J. M. Kummerow, *Introduction to Type in Organizations*. Consulting Psychologists Press Inc. (1987). Obtainable from Oxford Psychologists Press.
3. W. Bridges, *The Character of Organizations: using Jungian Type in Organizational Development*. Consulting Psychologists Press Inc. (1992), p. vii. Obtainable from Oxford Psychologists Press.

Chapter 8
1. I. Briggs Myers, *Gifts Differing*, p. 154.

2. D. Keirsey and M. Bates, *Please Understand Me*, p. 97ff.

3. Meisgeier, Murphy and Meisgeier, *A Teacher's Guide to Type: A New Perspective on Individual Differences in the Classroom*. Consulting Psychologists Press Inc. (1989). Obtainable from Oxford Psychologists Press.

Chapter 9
1. R. M. Oswald and O. Kroeger, *Personality Type and Religious Leadership*. The Alban Institute, 4125 Nebraska Avenue NW, Washington DC, 20016 (1989).

2. ibid., p. 55.

Chapter 10
1. *The Vision*, Journal of the National Retreat Association, Liddon House, 24 South Audley Street, London W1Y 5DL.

2. C. Michael and M. Norrisey, *Prayer and Temperament*. The Open Door Inc., PO Box 866, Charlottesville, Virginia 22902 (1984). Obtainable from Oxford Psychologists Press.

3. R. Repicky OSB, 'Jungian Typology and Christian Spirituality' in *The Way*, vol 42 (1983).

4. ibid.

5. C. Michael and M. Norrisey, *Prayer and Temperament*, p. 94.

6. J. Biersdroft, *How Prayer Shapes Ministry*. The Alban Institute (1992).

Chapter 11
1. J. Provost, *The Type Reporter*, vol 3, no. 7 (1988) and vol. 4, no. 5 (1989).

Chapter 12
1. F. Wright Saunders, *Katharine and Isabel: Mother's Light, Daughter's Journey*. Consulting Psychologists Press Inc. (1991), p. 12. Obtainable from Oxford Psychologists Press.

2. ibid., p. 38.

3. ibid., p. 137.